San Francisco

Berlitz®
San Francisco

Text by Paula Tevis
Updated by Lisa Crovo
Edited by Media Content Marketing, Inc.
Photography: Chris Coe except pages 3, 4, 6,
64, 68, 76, 98 by Doug Traverso
Cover photograph by Chris Coe
Photo Editor: Naomi Zinn
Layout: Media Content Marketing, Inc.
Cartography by Ortelius Design
Managing Editor: Tony Halliday

Eighth Edition 2002 (Reprinted 2004)

CONTACTING THE EDITORS
Every effort has been made to provide accurate information in this publication, but
changes are inevitable. The publisher cannot be responsible for any resulting loss,
inconvenience or injury. We would appreciate it if readers would call our attention
to any errors or outdated information by contacting Berlitz Publishing, PO Box 7910,
London SE1 1WE, England. Fax: (44) 20 7403 0290;
e-mail: berlitz@apaguide.co.uk; www.berlitzpublishing.com

CONTENTS

● A 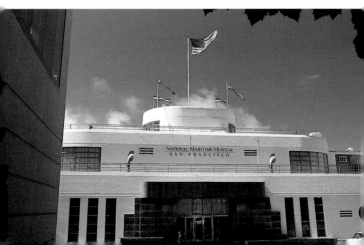 in the text denotes a highly recommended sight

San Francisco

THE CITY AND ITS PEOPLE

Earthquakes aside, there's just no shaking off San Francisco. One of America's favorite cities, San Francisco clings to your soul, as irresistibly as a yen for the good things in life, or a song that won't vacate your head. The ballad may be syrupy, but so many millions of people have left their hearts in San Francisco that you can't fight it: The City by the Bay incites love at first sight – a love that lasts.

The first astonishment is the setting. So many thrillers have been filmed in San Francisco that the hills look as familiar as home; and yet it turns out that the cameramen didn't need trick lenses; the hills are just as giddily steep as in the movies. Officially, 43 hills stand up to be counted, most famously Nob, Russian, Telegraph, and Twin Peaks. From these vantage points the views are endlessly varied and stimulating – the magnificent Pacific, the choppy bay and its mysterious islands, and other hills dotted with mansions, eccentric Victorian houses, or skyscrapers with character. And if somewhere in the world there is a more noble bridge than the Golden Gate, its glory isn't crowned with wisps of fog.

The sound of a foghorn is as much a San Francisco particular as the clang of a cable car bell. First heard in the 1870s, that bell still incites the squeals of tourists hanging on as the cable car rounds a bend. More subtly, you can hear the actual cable speeding under the street at a relentless 9$\frac{1}{2}$ mph (15 km/h), perpetually protesting like a distant alarm clock. A more piercing aural trademark is the tweet of the tin whistle of a hotel doorman commanding a taxi in the sunshine, or pleading for one in the drizzle. In ethnic neighborhoods the sounds are as exotic as the hiss of a North Beach espresso machine or the slurping of soba noodles in Japantown.

Even in summer – more so in summer, when much of California is broiling – the San Francisco weather is invigorating. Thanks to a temperate marine climate, as it's called, the mercury rarely tops 70°F (21°C) at any time of year. Thus, except for the more arduous hills, which are best tackled by cable car or bus, San Francisco is definitely a city for walkers. How else could you appreciate the architectural adventure of the high skyscrapers in the Financial District, the abundance of Italian cafés in North Beach, or the pungent aromas of Chinatown?

San Francisco has always been a melting pot, especially since international fortune-hunters flooded in to exploit the gold rush of the mid-19th century. At the moment, the largest single ethnic group in the city is Chinese, though every culture in the world seems to be represented, as evidenced by the mushrooming roster of ethnic restaurants, from Afghani to Vietnamese.

Home-grown Americans from all parts of the country keep moving in, attracted by the scenery, the eternal springtime, and a truly cosmopolitan atmosphere in a city of fewer than three-quarters of a million people. Another intangible inducement is a very civilized tolerance. San Francisco respects its minorities of all stripes, including starving artists, splinter-party politicians, and militant homosexuals.

All this is going on in a relatively compact corner of the West Coast, the tip of the peninsula. It is here that the city and county of San Francisco, which coincide, cover about 46 square miles (120 sq. km) – one-tenth of the area of Los Angeles. To put San Francisco into a more metropolitan context, the region is considered to include Oakland, San Jose, and the rest of the nine-county Bay Area, totaling 6 million people. Even so, the resident population is outnumbered by the annual tourist influx by a ratio of more than two to one.

San Francisco Bay, a naval, commercial, and recreational haven of 496 square miles (1,285 sq. km), went undiscovered until rather late in the colonization of America. For a couple of centuries, Spanish, Portuguese, and English sailors must have sailed on past the Golden Gate, where the Pacific meets the bay, but it seems to have been fogbound every time. Finally, in 1769, the Spanish pioneer Gaspar de Portolá exclaimed over a harbor big enough to shelter all the navies of Europe. It was a sort of backdoor discovery, for his party stumbled

San Francisco caters well to its many visitors, and there are lots of ways to see the sights.

on the bay from land, not sea. Seven years later Spanish colonists arrived and set up a fort to defend the bay, and built a mission to convert the local Native Americans. Mission Dolores, which is still here, was dedicated to St. Francis of Assisi, or, as they say in Spanish, San Francisco.

By 1846, when the town, then ruled by Mexico, was claimed by the United States, there was nothing much to brag about – a trading post with fewer than a thousand inhabitants. Two years later, a revolution was sparked by a four-letter word: gold. The bonanza on the American River, 140 miles (225 km) away, catapulted San Francisco to the status of an international dream. And there was no looking back. The Barbary Coast was eventually tamed, but the idea of a land of limitless opportunity still persisted. Even today, with omnipresent panhandlers reminding tourists of grim contemporary social problems, an overriding optimism wafts in with the tangy Pacific breeze.

The threat of earthquakes is all too real for the people of San Francisco, as everyone was tragically reminded in 1989, when the city trembled at a shrug of the San Andreas Fault. Seismological phenomena are a fact of life in California, where some people wait for the Big One with the fatalism of a fisherman in a typhoon.

The earthquake of October 1989, shown "live" on television from Candlestick (3Com) Park during the baseball World Series, was far less terrible than the catastrophe of 1906 that became the great dividing line in San Francisco's history. On that occasion thousands of men, women, and children lost their lives, fires burned for three days, and the city was all but wiped out.

Many hundreds of Victorian landmarks were preserved or restored, but what replaced the rubble was an elegant 20th-century city, worthy of its position as unofficial capital of the American West. (Los Angeles has since overtaken San Francisco in population and power,

Nothing says San Francisco quite like its attractive Victorian homes.

Ferries come and go at busy Pier 39, taking passengers to Alcatraz and around the bay for a famous view or two.

although, according to most visitors, L.A. offers little competition when it comes to charm.) Culture is thriving in San Francisco, with its opera, symphony orchestra, ballet, theaters, museums, and universities, and spills over into the areas of refined shopping and eating.

Like its setting and its history, San Francisco is romantic, but with so much to see and do, the pace can become hectic. For relief, cross the bay to the heavenly sanctuary of the redwoods, the sunny valleys of vineyards, or waterside villages that seem more Mediterranean than Californian. On the return journey, soak up the mood of the harbor, its islands, sailboats, and ferries, and the San Francisco skyline, a thrilling clash of high-rise majesty, low-slung homes, and sprinkles of parkland. If there were nothing here but 43 bare hills, it would still be a marvel.

A BRIEF HISTORY

Until the American Revolution, the San Francisco Bay Area, isolated by ocean and mountains, languished in prehistoric obscurity. While 18th-century Bostonians were going to Harvard, humming the catchy music of the young Mozart, the inhabitants of this region were fishing and trapping. They were Native Americans of the Ohlone (Costanoan) and Mivok tribes, so far removed from modern influences that they had never seen a horse or a wheel.

Not until 1776 did the first colonists – the Spanish – arrive at what is now San Francisco, where they built a presidio, or military garrison, and a religious mission to convert and educate the Indians. Settlement began seven years after the first Europeans had discovered the mighty bay. Ships from many European nations, sailing up and down the Pacific coast, had been missing the Golden Gate for centuries, probably because of the fog. The best-known explorer to come close was Sir Francis Drake, who is said to have landed farther north in 1579 at what is now Drake's Bay. He claimed everything in sight for England, but nobody took any notice.

In the early years the Spanish colony showed no particular promise. The Presidio, overlooking the Golden Gate, was never called on to repel invaders, and so unimpressive were the defenses that the commander was reprimanded during the late 1700s when he twice entertained the captain of a visiting British Royal Navy ship, thus disclosing his unpreparedness.

Meanwhile, inland, the mission went about its evangelical work, but many Indians died before they could be forced to convert, as European diseases rampaged through their population.

Mexicans and Gringos

California came under Mexican control in 1822, when Mexico won its independence from Spain. A few years later the new regime secularized the network of California missions, including Mission Dolores. The church's extensive lands were reassigned to settlers, some of whom amassed huge cattle ranches. With the Franciscan friars out of a job, the native Indians tragically lost direction, caught halfway between the old and the new civilizations.

While the Presidio was impressing nobody and the mission was declining, a live-wire English sea captain, William Richardson, founded a more promising settlement – starting with his own tent – near the sheltered Yerba Buena Cove. The cove disappeared long ago as landfills pushed back the sea from hills considered too steep to make settlements on. In fact, the site of Richardson's tent is now high and dry in the middle of Chinatown.

The American era began on 9 July 1846, in the early stages of the Mexican War, when the *U.S.S. Portsmouth* sailed through the Golden Gate. The sloop's captain,

Mission Dolores recalls the city's early days under Spanish colonial rule.

John Montgomery, led a party ashore and raised the Stars and Stripes flag over the plaza, now called Portsmouth Square after the ship. The ship's cannon then saluted the change of proprietorship. Captain Montgomery himself is immortalized in the name of Montgomery Street in the Financial District.

The peace treaty of Guadalupe Hidalgo was signed on 2 February 1848, only nine days after gold was discovered in California.

Bonanza!

The starter's gun for California's lusty gold rush was fired far from civilization, halfway between Sacramento and Lake Tahoe. At a lumber mill in the Sierra foothills, a carpenter named James Marshall glimpsed the sparkle of the first nugget on 24 January 1848. His boss, the pioneering

City Planners

The layout of San Francisco's streets – grandly logical, on paper – goes back to the early days of Yerba Buena. In 1839 a Swiss settler, Jean-Jacques Vioget, was drafted to draw up a scheme for a town. He based his plan on the Spanish model of a large town square from which streets radiated in a grid.

Under American rule in 1847, an Irish surveyor, Jasper O'Farrell, was given the project of extending the plan. He "invented" Market Street and the much bigger blocks to the south. Both planners were more interested in theory than in practice, which is why the city's long, straight streets go over the tops of hills instead of circling around them. O'Farrell's additional gift to modern motorists is the struggle to find a way to cross Market Street.

tycoon John Augustus Sutter, helped with chemical tests confirming that this was the genuine 23-carat article. Breaking their conspiratorial silence, Sutter soon spread the word.

At first, the reaction in San Francisco was skeptical. Then an ironmonger and huckster, Sam Brannan, appeared in the center of town with a bottle of nuggets, shouting, "Gold! Gold from the American River!" By no coincidence, his sales of shovels and pickaxes picked up instantly. Brannan went on to become the city's first millionaire. Gold, then silver, made San Francisco the capital of the American West.

The city was virtually abandoned overnight as every ambitious, able-bodied citizen rushed to the gold fields. They were followed by the so-called "Forty-Niners," eager prospectors lured from as far away as Australia, China, and Europe. Thousands more boarded ships in New York for the daunting four- to six-month voyage around the tip of South America to San Francisco. On arrival, many a sailor jumped ship at San Francisco and joined the rush for the "Mother of all Lodes."

The population of the shanty-town of San Francisco doubled overnight, then doubled again. In a few months an overgrown hamlet of 2,000 people became a rugged city of 20,000. Before the gold rush fizzled, hundreds of thousands of hopefuls had passed through San Francisco, enriching every entrepreneur from bootmaker to brothel-keeper. It was a wild time, with shortages of everything – housing, food, and law and order – the perfect climate for fast profits.

Real estate speculators, gamblers, and money-lenders prospered much more handsomely than the miners, especially an immigrant from Germany, one Levi Strauss, who

This statue of firemen, which stands in North Beach, marks a vulnerable side of the city, namely its devastation by fire.

unloaded excess fabric in the form of denim trousers that stood up to the hardships of the Sierra: Levi's jeans.

Golden State

California was coining precious metals so fast that the US Congress granted it statehood in 1850, skipping the intermediate dependent status of territory. After the gold ran out, a bonanza of silver, known as the Comstock Lode, followed. Providing the mining equipment and infrastructure for the Virginia City adventure, San Francisco became the fourth-busiest port in the nation, a real town with cultural landmarks like hotels, theaters, and hundreds of saloons and other recreational facilities.

Like many another boom town, San Francisco suffered the side-effects of its prosperity: overcrowding, crime, immorality, and exploitation. It was also a time of disastrous fires, many the work of arsonists. With its haphazardly built shacks and tents, fragile oil lamps, and a tendency for windiness, the town was extremely vulnerable to fire. Crime was also a cause for concern, and the citizens rallied with vigilante groups. If this resulted in the odd lynching, San Franciscans chalked it up to a worthy trend toward an orderly society.

San Francisco drew closer to the rest of the United States in the 1860s with the opening of a direct telegraph line to New York and, at the end of the decade, of the rail link that joined the Atlantic to the Pacific. Four Sacramento merchants, whose names are still affixed to California institutions, joined forces to build the Central Pacific railroad. They were Charles Crocker, Collis P. Huntington, Mark Hopkins,

Chinese on the Railway

The Chinese gold miners who came to California after the 1849 rush were treated coolly, often cruelly, by Americans and Europeans working the Mother Lode. Opportunity beckoned anew during the construction of the transcontinental railway. The Central Pacific found that the Chinese were the best laborers for laying track through hair-raising mountain terrain. Eventually, more than eight out of ten workers on the line were Chinese laborers. Once the project was finished, unemployed Chinese flooded the California job market, prompting more discrimination. Most of the Chinese stopped trying to compete and retreated to their own enclave, San Francisco's Chinatown. Still, there were anti-Chinese riots in 1875, as well as the passing of the Chinese Exclusion Act in 1882.

and Leland Stanford. Their scheme, generously subsidized by the US government, finally came to fruition at Promontory, Utah, in May 1869, when the "golden spike" symbolically spliced eastern and western lines. The "Big Four" entrepreneurs profited a great deal from their monopoly, and the railroad opened the way for unemployed Easterners to descend on the golden West, thus depressing wages, prices, and the economy in general.

Growing Up

In the 1870s and 1880s, San Francisco took on the air of a real city, the key to the West, with a population in the hundreds of thousands and amenities to match. Work on Golden Gate Park, destined to become one of the nation's biggest and best municipal parks, was begun in 1870. City transport took a great leap forward in 1873 when the first cable cars made Nob Hill effortlessly attainable. Next, trolleys brought the more distant areas within reach, and land prices boomed.

The financial prowess of the city was confirmed when a stately United States Mint was built at Fifth and Mission streets. The granite fortress processed a fortune in gold and silver from area mines, producing coins that filled the banks (and pockets) of the West. The Pacific Coast Stock Exchange was founded in 1875, as was a hotel worthy of any tycoon. San Francisco's Palace Hotel, built at a cost of five million dollars, could hold its own with any luxury establishment in the country. Seven stories high, with 800 rooms around an atrium to which guests were conducted in great style, the Palace entertained financiers, statesmen, victorious generals, and other celebrities. Among other elements of modern design, it was meant to be earthquake-proof. Memories of an earthquake during the Civil War period were still resonant.

Falling Down

As San Francisco slept, early on the morning of 18 April 1906, the clocks stopped at 5:12. If there had been a Richter Scale in those days, it would have registered about 8.3. The Great San Francisco Earthquake fissured streets, toppled chimneys, and crumbled thousands of houses, but the worst was yet to come. As gas mains broke, fires erupted – but the water mains also ruptured. The San Francisco Fire Department, whose chief was one of the first victims, could do little to control the flames. The great fire roared out of control for 3 days and wiped out 4 square miles (10 sq. km) of the heart of the city. Crowded aboard ferries heading for Oakland and Marin County, the city's refugees looked back at an apocalyptic skyline under a pall of black smoke.

The Presidio mobilized federal soldiers to control the uncontrollable. They were ordered to dynamite buildings to provide fire breaks, but their knowledge of explosives, and fires, was minimal. During the disaster, the army's miscalculations managed to burn down Chinatown and other tightly packed neighborhoods. Soldiers and National Guardsmen were also assigned to law-and-order duties, resulting in further casualties in the effort to discourage looting. The death toll was between three and five thousand.

With a quarter of a million San Franciscans homeless, most of them camped out in Golden Gate Park, the pressure to re-build was staggering. Thanks to help from all over the world, reconstruction pushed ahead, and within three years the disaster area had been reclaimed. A clean-up of a different sort brought the downfall of the corrupt regime of Mayor Eugene Schmitz, although His Honor himself managed to avoid jail. Abe Ruef, the power behind city hall, earned himself 14 years at San Quentin prison for extortion.

To demonstrate to the entire world that recovery was complete, the Panama-Pacific International Exposition was held in San Francisco in 1915. It celebrated the opening of the Panama Canal, but more than that the rebirth of a great city. When the tourists had all gone home, the Barbary Coast night life scene – shameless by any standard – was finally tamed under the state legislature's red-light abatement law. With a population of half a million, San Francisco had come a long way from the days of the Wild West.

During the Depression local artists were employed to paint frescoes inside Coit Tower.

Depression and War

During the Great Depression of the 1930s, ambitious public-works projects were designed to provide employment for workers with many skills. The interior of the Coit Tower on Telegraph Hill, dedicated in 1933, was adorned with frescoes by local artists; Franklin Roosevelt's New Deal paid their salaries. The 1930s also put brawnier workers on the payroll, constructing two great bridges: the San Francisco-Oakland Bay Bridge, and the much shorter, but more glamorous, Golden Gate Bridge. The two opened only six months apart. In a mood of growing optimism, yet another San Francisco World's Fair, the Golden

Gate International Exposition, was held on reclaimed land in the bay, subsequently dubbed Treasure Island.

The biggest job-provider of all, World War II, came soon enough. The threat to San Francisco was perceived to be real, and the city staged its first blackout alert only one day after the Japanese attack on Pearl Harbor, in December 1941. The next summer a nervous US government rounded up Japanese residents (including third-generation American citizens) and moved them to the isolation and hardship of internment camps. To try to prove their patriotism, more than 30,000 Japanese-Americans volunteered to fight, and their US Army regiment became the most decorated in the history of American combat.

San Francisco was to play a big part in the war effort as a military and industrial base. As hundreds of Liberty ships rolled from Bay Area assembly lines, 1.6 million American fighting men were funneled through Fort Mason on ships heading for the combat zones. After Japan surrendered in 1945, the U.N. Charter was signed in San Francisco.

Bohemians

San Francisco had always had more than its fair share of non-conformists; the new breeds evolving after the war provoked the world's fascination if not admiration.

First came the Beat Generation, later known disparagingly as "beatniks" (the word was coined after their heyday by the late *Chronicle* columnist Herb Caen). Congregating in North Beach *(see page 44)*, they dressed like revolutionaries, drank coffee while discussing philosophy, read and wrote poetry (some memorable), and supported avant-garde jazz.

In the 1960s the action shifted to the low-rent Haight-Ashbury district *(see page 58)*, where a new species of rebel, less productive intellectually, came to be called "hippies." Ideological powerhouses in San Francisco and Berkeley inspired student radicals all over the United States with their demonstrations for improved civil rights and against American involvement in the Vietnam war.

After the US pulled out of Vietnam, San Francisco's image as a hotbed of radicalism re-focused on a wave of gay rights agitation. In 1978, the first official in the US to proclaim his homosexuality, City Supervisor Harvey Milk, was assassinated, along with Mayor George Moscone. A lenient sentence for the assassin – a disaffected politician – spurred violent protests. The new mayor was a woman – Dianne Feinstein – who would serve 10 years in the post before being elected to the US Senate.

Shaken Again

Earth tremors are a familiar phenomenon in California, but the quake that struck on 17 October 1989 demanded that everyone take notice – in fact, millions of viewers were watching the beginnings of the World Series relayed from San Francisco when the earth shook. Registering 7.1 on the Richter Scale, it was the most severe tremor since 1906, causing billions of dollars' worth of damage and claiming 67 lives. Earthquake-proof modern buildings survived, but many older houses suffered and a large section of the double-decker Bay Bridge collapsed. The elevated two-tier Embarcadero Freeway was damaged as well, and the eyesore was subsequently dismantled after a contentious debate. In a fitting bit of irony, the earthquake can be credited for liberating a long-ignored corner of the city in the decade that followed, paving the way for waterfront development, additional public transportation routes, and a brand-new ballpark.

Historical Landmarks

1769 Spanish soldier José Ortega discovers San Francisco Bay while on a scouting mission for Gaspar de Portolá, governor of Spanish California.

1776 On June 29, the first Mass is conducted in San Francisco on the site of Mission Dolores.

1835 William A. Richardson becomes Yerba Buena's first official resident when he erects a shelter in what is now Chinatown.

1846 During the war with Mexico, Captain John B. Montgomery arrives at the site of today's Portsmouth Square and claims Yerba Buena for the United States.

1847 Yerba Buena renamed San Francisco.

1848 James Marshall discovers gold in the Sierra Nevada foothills prompting the great gold rush of 1849.

1873 Andrew Hallidie's cable car takes its inaugural run down Clay Street on August 2.

1906 Two tremors hit San Francisco in the early morning followed by three days of fire. The city is virtually destroyed.

1912 The San Francisco Municipal Railway is created, one of the first publicly owned transit companies in the nation.

1915 The city hosts the Panama-Pacific International Exposition.

1936–1937 The San Francisco-Oakland Bay Bridge opens in 1936, followed in 1937 by the Golden Gate Bridge.

1945 The United Nations charter is signed by representatives from 50 countries in the War Memorial Opera House on 26 June.

1967 Golden Gate Park is the site for the "Human Be-In" and the Haight-Ashbury neighborhood becomes a draw for hippies.

1978 Former city supervisor Dan White assassinates Mayor George Moscone and gay City Supervisor Harvey Milk.

1989 A 7.1 earthquake hits the city during the World Series baseball game.

2000 A new Muni route down the Embarcadero to Fisherman's Wharf opens after two years of construction. The San Francisco Giants baseball team plays its first season at Pacific Bell Park.

WHERE TO GO

From the social summit of Nob Hill to the ethnic patchwork of the Richmond District, the neighborhoods of San Francisco have their own distinct personalities. If you were lost in the retro Haight-Ashbury district, you'd certainly get the impression it wasn't tidy Noe Valley. Meanwhile, Russian Hill and the Mission District are as different as New York's Upper East Side is from the Lower East Side.

With its well-oiled if oft maligned public transportation system, all of San Francisco is easy to reach. And once you're in the neighborhood you want, it's a great walking town. Walking tours proliferate, targeted at a broad spectrum of interests, from the historical and architectural to the literary or ethnic.

However, before you start off, it's wise to get your bearings with a half-day coach tour. Considering all the hills and the fact that the city is surrounded on three sides by water, its geographical subtleties are not instantly apparent; many a first-time visitor, admiring the steel span of the Bay Bridge, thinks that it's the Golden Gate. Another worthwhile orientation exercise is a one-hour harbor tour, featuring views of the San Francisco skyline.

For the price of an all-day Muni pass you can see a great deal of the city using buses, street cars, and cable cars. Driving around in traffic-heavy San Francisco is not recommended, and locating a parking place is only for the most determined of individuals.

So many hotels, shops, and attractions are centered in Union Square that we begin our survey of San Francisco's sights here. You might want to do the same, as the Visitor Information Center of the San Francisco Convention & Visitors Bureau is right at hand *(see page 122)*, near the

Powell Street cable car terminus in Hallidie Plaza at Market and Powell streets. They can supply you with brochures, maps, and answers to your questions.

DOWNTOWN

Union Square

London has Regent Street, and New York Fifth Avenue. San Francisco does its fashionable shopping around **Union Square**. The names that glitter here stimulate shoppers internationally: Tiffany's, Saks Fifth Avenue, Macy's, Neiman-Marcus, Cartier, and Gucci. In recent years a new crop of stores, including Nike Town and Levis, have joined such hot spots as Virgin Megastore to take the staid edge off Union Square.

Ever surrounded by slow-moving traffic, including a cable-car line, Union Square is a formally landscaped downtown park that sits right on top of the nation's first underground parking structure. The great statue of Victory on top of the Corinthian column in the center of Union Square celebrates Admiral Dewey's 1898 Manila Bay win during the Spanish-American war.

A landmark on the west side of the square, the **Westin St. Francis Hotel**, first opened for business in 1904. Rebuilt, overhauled, ex-

Union Square, where you can shop till you drop or simply stroll in the park.

Have yourself an adventure in Chinatown, 24 blocks wide and a world away.

panded, and refurbished over the years (the new lobby alone cost $2 million in 1991), the hotel has welcomed many royals, heads of government, and celebrities. Dozens of hotels, from five-star palaces to modest rooms with shared facilities, are found within a 5-minute walk of Union Square. The area is also populated with many of San Francisco's homeless, who make their quiet appeal to the consciences of the city's well-heeled passers-by.

On the east side of the square, **Maiden Lane** runs into Stockton Street. The prim name is an affectation. Maiden Lane was once known as Morton Street, under which alias it was a hotbed of Barbary Coast vice. The post-earthquake fire of 1906 extinguished the red lights, and nowadays it's a pleasant and well-appointed pedestrian street of designer shops.

The building at 140 Maiden Lane is the only San Francisco work by the architect Frank Lloyd Wright. The ramp is reminiscent of Wright's revolutionary Guggenheim Museum in New York.

☛ Chinatown

Immerse yourself totally in the experience and lose yourself in the 24-square-block confines of San Francisco's Chinatown. Here the second biggest Chinese community outside Asia (New York's is first) crowds into the exotic emporia, temples, tea houses, and restaurants that are so good the residents of Canton would be jealous. By way of infrastructure there are Chinese banks, schools, law offices, travel agencies, video shops, bookstores, laundries, and factories recalling the sweatshops of earlier times.

Since gold rush days, most of the Chinese in San Francisco, and the United States in general, have had their roots in Guangdong (Kwangtung) province, whose capital is Canton. Thus the Cantonese dialect and cuisine are often encountered here. But newer immigrants from other Chinese provinces, and from Indochina, Hong Kong, and Taiwan, have added their own distinctive flavor to the melting pot.

In order to enter Chinatown through the front door, approach it from the Union Square area or the Financial District. The **Chinatown Gate**, at Grant Avenue and Bush Street, has the classic design of a Chinese village gate, but it

Waiting for the Big One

San Francisco sits right on top of the San Andreas Fault, a major fracture in the earth's crust that runs northwest from the Gulf of California for 600 miles (965 km), passing beneath the city and separating Point Reyes from the mainland. The BART subway tunnel between San Francisco and Oakland was bored right through the fault.

The Baja California peninsula and the coast to the west of the fault are moving north relative to the rest of North America, at an average of half an inch (1 cm) per year. There has been no movement along the San Francisco section of the fault since the disastrous earthquake of 1906, but experts predict that there's a 50/50 chance of another major quake – the dreaded Big One – occurring within the next 30 years.

27

dates from 1970. Bulging with souvenir shops and restaurants, always bustling Grant Avenue is the prime tourist promenade of Chinatown. But be sure to veer off to find a more authentic experience on Broadway and Stockton Street.

Two blocks ahead, across the California Street cable car tracks, **Old St. Mary's Church** was San Francisco's Roman Catholic cathedral during most of the second half of the 19th century. Now it is a parish church. Under the clock is an inscription, "Son Observe the Time and Fly from Evil." That's "son," not "sun" – it was aimed at prospective patrons of the brothels that used to operate across the street.

Portsmouth Square, where slow-motion *tai chi* exercises are performed and where old men play checkers, happens to be very important historically. This was the main plaza of the original Mexican colony that became San Francisco. The square sits atop a parking garage and features a children's playground, benches, and a perfect view of the Transamerica Pyramid in the Financial District.

The **Bank of Canton** at 743 Washington Street preserves the delightful **Old Chinese Telephone Exchange** in the original, spectacularly Chinese setting of red pillars and soaring tile roofs. This was the headquarters of the Chinatown telephone exchange, where operators could deal with subscribers in English as well as in Chinese dialects. After World War II the arrival of dial telephones put these talented linguists out of work.

The back streets of San Francisco's Chinatown meet almost all specifications for those in search of the mysteries of the Far East. Typically, **Ross Alley**, up Washington Street from Grant Avenue, is both exotic and, since the 1980s, nicely paved. The little shops and factories are just what you'd expect to find in an alley beyond the tourist zone of Kowloon – garment factories, jewelry shops, sellers of miniature

Formerly known as the Old Chinese Telephone Exchange, this delightful building is now home to the Bank of Canton.

Buddhist shrines, and a one-chair barber shop. Here, too, is the Golden Gate Fortune Cookie Company, from where those typically American-Chinese pastries originate. Watch the deft hands of the operators folding moist cookies around slips of paper enigmatically foretelling the fate of future customers at Chinese restaurants around the world. You can purchase bags of fresh almond or fortune cookies from the ladies in the factory.

Although Grant Avenue constantly teems with tourists, **Stockton Street** is busier still; it's where the Chinese community shop for food and essentials. Soak up the sights, sounds, and smells of Chinese supermarkets, open-air vegetable markets, fish markets, herbalists, delicatessens, pastry shops, and tea rooms. On the roof of the modern Chinatown branch of the US Post Office at Stockton and Clay streets is a Chinese temple – the **Kong Chow Temple** – with a historic altar and a view of the bay from its balcony. At 843 Stockton Street, the headquarters of the **Chinese Six Companies** (officially the Chinese Consolidated Benevolent Association) is a garishly decorated building dating from the early 20th century. The organization was central to the fight against anti-Chinese discrimination, which persisted until relatively recent times.

Financial District and Jackson Square

Heading northeast into the Financial District, stop in the **Crocker Galleria**, an airy, glass-domed shopping mall on three floors. It was inspired by Milan's Galleria Vittorio Emanuelle, built more than a century earlier. Across Sutter Street from the mall, don't miss the **Hallidie Building**, named after the man who put the cable car on track. Dating from 1917, it might have been the first "glass curtain wall" building anywhere; the glass-and-metal façade hangs from the top instead of helping to support the structure. Apart from the boldness of the engineering, there are wonderful frills, such as the disguised external fire escapes. The ground floor of the Hallidie Building is now shared by a bank and a post office. Office workers take their lunch breaks on **Belden Place**, off Bush Street between Pine and Kearny streets. Here, a half dozen delicious restaurants offer outdoor dining Monday through Saturday until 10pm.

Place names in San Francisco tend to be straightforward, but just as North Beach is not a beach, **Jackson Square** is not a square. The name refers to a block of buildings bounded by Jackson, Montgomery, Gold, and Sansome streets, just north of the Transamerica Pyramid. The city's pioneers crudely reclaimed this area from the bay with ballast from arriving ships, and in many cases the ships themselves, abandoned by crewmen who joined the gold rush. This was destined to become one of the most infamous areas of the Barbary Coast. A relatively small collection of low-rise, thick-walled brick offices, banks, shops, and factories miraculously withstood the quake and subsequent fires in 1906. In the middle of the 20th century, when the district's historic and architectural importance was discovered, restoration of the landmarks began. Today, Jackson Square has become the elegant place to have a law office, ad agency, art gallery, or antiques shop.

BESIDE THE BAY

San Francisco's big, beautiful waterfront has undergone a facelift. It began when the 1989 earthquake doomed the elevated Embarcadero Freeway, an eyesore that cost nearly half as much to dismantle as it had to build. With the demise of the "abominable autobahn," as the San Francisco *Chronicle* called it at the outset, unobstructed views of the Ferry Building and harbor were revealed, and local developers and planners took a long, hard look around. By now, the construction crews have gone home, leaving a length of new Muni tracks and inviting plazas on which to linger while you admire the imported palm trees that

Fresh produce and a fresh ocean breeze quayside, at The Embarcadero.

Spanning San Francisco and Oakland, the Bay Bridge is often mistaken for the Golden Gate by visitors.

decorate the boulevard. Called **The Embarcadero** (Spanish for "quay"), this piece of the bay stretches from the new baseball stadium at King Street all the way to Fisherman's Wharf.

Rumbling almost overhead near Harrison Street you'll get a dramatic view of the **San Francisco-Oakland Bay Bridge.** The bridge, anchored in the middle on Yerba Buena Island, is 8 miles (13 km) long. Like the more celebrated Golden Gate Bridge, it was built during the Depression days of the 1930s. Unlike the Golden Gate, the Bay Bridge wears a necklace of lights to add to the romance of San Francisco's nights.

Just northwest of the bridge's take-off for Oakland is the **Ferry Building**, where you may board a Golden Gate commuter ferry to Sausalito. The station and its multi-stage tower date from the turn of the 20th century. The Embarcadero is a very mixed bag between the Ferry Building and Fisherman's Wharf. Walkers, joggers, bicyclists, and skate boarders make the most of its wide sidewalks. The maritime activities that made this a great port, such as whaling and countless, varied ferries, have either disappeared or moved to the railhead at Oakland across the bay. What's left are the occasional luxury liner welcoming passengers bound for Alaska, harbor cruise ships, sightseeing boats, and deep-sea fishing charters.

Fisherman's Wharf

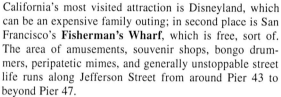

California's most visited attraction is Disneyland, which can be an expensive family outing; in second place is San Francisco's **Fisherman's Wharf**, which is free, sort of. The area of amusements, souvenir shops, bongo drummers, peripatetic mimes, and generally unstoppable street life runs along Jefferson Street from around Pier 43 to beyond Pier 47.

Pier 39, a tourist complex constructed of recycled lumber from old wharves, is the major draw, with millions of visitors a year. They come to shop, snack or dine, watch street performers, ride a double-deck carousel, admire the view of the bay, take a tour, rent a yacht, or discover what all that

---

Persistent Pinnipeds

The bewhiskered sea lions have been barking at Pier 39 since 1990, evidently attracted by a herring bonanza and a totally safe, comfortable haven. Although the big fellows put a potentially profitable yacht-parking zone out of action, nobody could convince them to leave, and federal law forbids harassing them. Pier 39 discovered that the smelly squatters were good for business; a sculpture was commissioned as a tribute to the blubbery marine mammals, and for tourists who want to know more about their swimming, feeding, and breeding habits, there are explanatory tours.

barking is about. No, that's not a pack of eager hounds on K-Dock, but up to 600 sea lions preening themselves and arguing over the best spot to sunbathe.

At the heart of it all is a concentration of fish restaurants. Exacting local gourmets may look down on them, citing that their prices are quite high for preparations that are quite pedestrian. Nevertheless, they're handy places for fresh local and imported seafood with a view. The "fast food" offered by outdoor stalls here—shrimp and crab cocktails, and clam chowder in an edible bowl—is popular, but if crab isn't in season (November through May), those crustaceans you're eating have been frozen. The truth is, the fishing fleet that you can survey here (the oldest boats are more prominently placed) contributes only a small percentage of the catch needed to feed all of San Francisco.

At Pier 45, a boat of a different sort is worth a look. *U.S.S. Pampanito,* a World War II submarine credited with the sinking of six Japanese ships, is open to visitors (admission is charged). Even though the sub is not submerged, some landlubbers feel a touch of claustrophobia in the narrow passages and dimly lit operations center.

Also moored here at Pier 45 is the Liberty Ship *S.S. Jeremiah O'Brien,* a veteran of the famous D-Day

Sea lions have taken up residence – and stolen the show – at Pier 39.

invasion of France and a memorial to the World War II personnel of the US Merchant Marine. More than 2,700 such ships were produced between 1941 and 1945.

Inland from Fisherman's Wharf, the **Cannery** occupies a vast red-brick building from the early 20th century. It was an important fruit-packing plant, cleverly converted into an attractive browsing, eating, and entertainment area, including a small museum of local history.

Ghirardelli Square is a bigger shopping and eating zone in a red-brick complex that began as a chocolate factory. A stylish alternative to the knick-knack-and-T-shirt boutiques of Jefferson Street, the enterprises here sell toys, jewelry, fashionable clothes, and even museum-worthy folk art from several continents, as well as chocolate—although the well-regarded local brand is now manufactured in a high-tech plant across the bay.

Victorian Park, overlooking the Aquatic Park Marina and the bay, is a pleasant place to break from the heavy footwork of sightseeing and shopping. Flocks of tourists spend more

Highway Robbery

Since its foundation in the middle of the 19th century, San Quentin has "entertained" many thousands of convicts, but few as colorful as C.E. Boles, alias "Black Bart." From 1875 to 1883 he specialized in holding up Wells Fargo stagecoaches – always politely, without firing a shot. Among the other ways he annoyed and embarrassed the law was to leave little poems at the scene of the crime, poems so bad that even Black Bart wrote, "And if for any cause I'm hung/Let it be for my verses." Traced by the laundry mark on a handkerchief he dropped, the gentlemanly desperado drew seven years at San Quentin. He was out in four: good behavior, of course.

time than they had planned in this park, queuing up for the cable car. This is where the Powell-Hyde line is pushed onto the turntable before heading back toward Union Square.

Farther along the beach, the **National Maritime Museum** is grandly titled, but is more remarkable for its building than for the exhibits, which are mostly model ships and photographs. It was built in 1939 in a streamlined design resembling a beached passenger ship, and there are appropriate nautical murals.

Real historic ships, rocking gently against the pier, are near at hand at **Hyde Street Pier**. More than a century old, the sidewheel ferry *Eureka* was the world's largest passenger-and-car ferry in its day. Vintage cars are parked aboard, as they were when the ferries constituted a link in US Highway 101. Other old ships that you can board include the *C.A. Thayer*, a three-masted lumber-carrying schooner, as well as *Balclutha*, a square-rigger launched in Scotland in 1886. Hyde Street Pier is so educational that even the toilets contain tableaux explaining the evolution of "heads" on ships, from the days when sailors had to "go" overboard.

Escape from Alcatraz

Officially, nobody ever escaped from Alcatraz. In all, 39 prisoners attempted it: 27 were caught, 7 were killed, and 5 have never been found but are assumed drowned.

In 1962, at the very end of the island's grim history, John Paul Scott made it to the San Francisco shore by greasing his body to help withstand the cold. A party of students found him clinging to the rocks at Fort Point, just below the Golden Gate Bridge, completely exhausted. Not knowing he was an escaped prisoner, they helpfully called the police to rescue the poor fellow in his hour of need.

The piers here are part of **Fort Mason**, which was head-quarters of the San Francisco Port of Embarkation during the Second World War. Over 1.5 million troops and 20 million tons of cargo passed through here on their way to combat zones. After the war, operations shifted to Oakland, and now the fort is part of the Golden Gate National Recreational Area.

At sea level, a complex of nine buildings is now devoted to entertainment, recreation, education, as well as other cultural initiatives. Three museums currently operate in the Fort Mason Center: the San Francisco Afro-American Historical and Cultural Society; the Italian Educational Cultural Center; and the San Francisco Museum of Craft and Folk Art. The Mexican Museum is now closed but will be moving to a new site near Yerba Buena Gardens in 2004.

Just a stone's throw from the city, Alcatraz saw many a prisoner attempt escape to San Francisco's seductive shores.

Alcatraz

All harbor excursions offer a close look at the moody former prison isle called **Alcatraz,** but the only way to step ashore and tour the abandoned cell-blocks is via the Blue and Gold Fleet from Pier 41. In summer and at weekends the tours are soon sold out; you have to book early, sometimes weeks ahead.

The vital difference between Alcatraz and its French equivalent, Devil's Island, is that Alcatraz looks out on a seductive city, not a hostile jungle; with the wind in the right direction, the prisoners could even hear the sounds of civilization just beyond their reach.

Alcatraz (from the Spanish *Isla de los Alcatraces,* or Pelican Island) served as America's most forbidding federal penitentiary from 1934 to 1963. It's said that Attorney General Robert Kennedy closed down the dilapidated prison when he discovered that it would have been cheaper (and certainly more comfortable) to keep the inmates at the Waldorf Astoria Hotel. Now the island is operated by the US National Park Service. A self-guided trail has been laid out, covering the principal areas of interest, or you can join in a more specialized walking tour led by a park ranger. Inside the cell-block, you can rent an audio tape (available in English, French, German, Italian, Japanese, and Spanish), on which tour directions are interspersed with a documentary based on the pertinent testimony of retired wardens and ex-prisoners. You'll see the cells of Al Capone and "the Birdman," Robert Stroud; roam the central corridor, ironically known as Broadway; have a chance to step inside a punishment cell; and check a typical menu in the dining hall. Alcatraz food is said to have been the best in the federal prison system– designed to give the inmates one less reason to riot.

By one count, 39 prisoners tried and failed to escape from the island. Two made it to the mainland, only to be picked up almost immediately, and five are listed as missing, officially presumed drowned – but did they? Here the imagination takes over.

Marina District

The earthquake of 1989 put the Marina on the world's television screens: Because the district is built on land reclaimed from the bay, dozens of houses succumbed to the 7.1 shock. The land was created from dredged sand after the 1906 quake to provide a site for the Panama-Pacific International Exposition of 1915.

Other than the earthquake problem, the Marina is a desirable place to live or visit, with its charming pastel-painted houses and varied up-market shopping on Chestnut Street. **Marina Green** is a fashionable bayside park for sunbathing, jogging, skating, biking, and kite flying.

An eye-catching monument from the 1915 World's Fair, the splendid pink **Palace of Fine Arts**, restored and reinforced, survived the tremor of 1989. This was a lucky development, for both its dreamy contribution to local

Pretty in pink – the Palace of Fine Arts dates from the 1915 World's Fair.

The tree-lined Presidio – the loveliest ex-military establishment you'll ever see.

pseudo-classical architecture, as well as its utility. The palace is now the site of the **Exploratorium**, also known as the Museum of Science, Art and Human Perception. Even an inquisitive octopus would not get his fill of "hands-on" exhibits at this endlessly instructive and entertaining center. Children become animated and intent, and parents and grandparents insist on their turn. Founded by Dr. Frank Oppenheimer (brother of the atomic Robert), the institution amounts to a big workshop.

The Presidio

Hundreds of thousands of invigorating cypress, eucalyptus, and pine trees shade the 1,480 acres (600 hectares) of the **Presidio** of San Francisco, the prettiest ex-military establishment you're ever likely to see. Founded as a Spanish fort in 1776, then active on the American side in several wars, it was belatedly converted to civilian life during the 1990s as part of the Golden Gate National Recreation Area. The beauty of the landscape dates from the late 19th century, when the trees were planted on what had been forbidding, rocky heights.

Feel free to explore the Presidio, either by bus or car or on foot, for its tastefully designed and impeccably maintained headquarters buildings, officers' quarters, and even model enlisted men's barracks.

The Presidio **museum**, at Lincoln Boulevard and Funston Avenue, is full of San Francisco military and civilian history. Once a hospital, it was built in 1864. A spacious military **cemetery** tells of battles going back to the Indian Wars. Not far away is an army pet cemetery, rich in anecdotal dog and cat gravestones.

Hiding under the southern end of the Golden Gate Bridge, mid-19th-century **Fort Point** is an ominous looking relic with a heart-stopping view of the strait. The National Park Service now runs tours through what was once the US Army's only brick fortress defending the West Coast against naval attack. The threat was considered real at the time of the Civil War, when it was suspected that the Confederate Navy might show up. As in so many military designs, this coastal artillery installation became out of date technologically as soon as it was built. Engineering enthusiasts will appreciate the almost-close-enough-to-touch view of the underside of the great bridge.

Golden Gate

Perhaps the bridge is thrilling because the pylons, as tall as 65-story buildings, taper upward like the spires of an Art

---

The Bridge: the Score

When it was built, the Golden Gate Bridge was the world's longest and tallest suspension structure. Here are some statistics:

Total length (including the approaches): 8,981 ft (2,737 m).

Height of towers: 746 ft (227 m).

Total weight on San Francisco pier foundation: 363,000 tons (329,000 metric tons).

Total length of wire in cables: 80,000 miles (129,000 km).

Traffic per year: 30 million vehicles.

Fare: $5 arriving in San Francisco; leaving town it's free.

Deco cathedral. It's not just the grace of its arches, though; you have to see the fog devouring its towers while the sun flashes on the water below, where sailboards zigzag in and out of the wake of ferryboats. Whatever the magic, one of America's favorite bridges is a wonder of engineering. In the little park at the southern end a statue honors the designer, Joseph B. Strauss of Chicago, also responsible for the Arlington Memorial Bridge in Washington DC.

Here you can see and touch a sample cross-section of one of the cables supporting the bridge – composed of 27,572 wires for a diameter of 3 ft (0.9 meters).

Chief Engineer Strauss began promoting the idea of a bridge in 1917. Many opponents of the project feared a bridge would deface the dramatic strait; others simply felt it couldn't be done, as tidal currents sometimes reach 60 mph (100 km/h). After "two decades and 200 million words," as Strauss put it, the people believed him. Construction began

in 1933. Eleven construction workers died, but 19 others were saved by the safety net Strauss designed. The bridge opened for traffic in May 1937.

A bridgeworker's job is never done, of course, so a crew of more than 40 is occupied year-round to clean and paint, using some 5,000 gallons (22,730 liters) of

Strolling across the Golden Gate is not for the faint of heart – you can feel it sway.

paint per year. The color, called "international orange," is the most easily visible in fog, and has won prizes for resisting salt, rain, sun, and wind.

Charles de Gaulle walked across the bridge in 1960. So can you, in either direction. It's about a 2-mile (3-km) trip – an invigorating, windy outing for the whole family. But leave behind anyone with a fear of heights; it's about 220 ft (67 m) straight down to the water, and you can feel the bridge swaying.

THE HILLS

The hills of San Francisco provide uplifting views of the city and the bay – just the thing for millionaires in search of a homestead or tourists merely wanting to borrow a panorama. Of the 40 or so hills available, we've chosen a few of the most appealing, with some detours into the valleys.

Telegraph Hill is named after the primitive semaphore set up here in gold rush days to relay news of ship arrivals to traders down in the Financial District. In 1876 a group of benefactors bought the top of the hill and gave it to the city for a park. Students of architecture and landscaping will be delighted to see how it turned out; the houses and gardens clinging to the hillsides are charmingly original. For a good look, walk the **Filbert Street steps** down to Sansome Street.

Sprouting from Telegraph Hill is landmark **Coit Tower**, a reinforced-concrete column of no practical value but considerable grace. Notwithstanding the version often recounted by tourist guides, it was not designed to resemble a fire-hose nozzle. It was merely an artful way of fulfilling the bequest of Lillie Hitchcock Coit, an unconventional 19th-century woman with close ties to the fire brigade, to build a beautiful monument. You have to pay to ride to the top for one of the best vantage points in town, but there is no charge to view the fine murals, which depict California life during the Great Depression years in Socialist Realist style, in the lobby.

North Beach

A landlocked valley between Telegraph Hill and Russian Hill, **North Beach** is not a beach at all. Although Chinatown is making inroads, this is the heart of the Italian community, where Columbus Day is a very big deal. North Beach is the place to find real Italian *prosciutto, gelato,* and *cappuccino*. It was once also the focus of the city's artistic and intellectual life, where poets and Bohemians attempted to influence the culture.

The center of the neighborhood is **Washington Square**, a small park with a bust of Benjamin Franklin in the middle. People from Chinatown arrive in the morning to do their martial arts exercises. The changing complexion of the area is also reflected in the **Church of Saints Peter and Paul**, where one of the morning masses is said in Chinese every Sunday.

North Beach's main street, Columbus Avenue, has several claims to fame. Lawrence Ferlinghetti's **City Lights Bookstore** was the headquarters of what became known as the Beat Generation, and earnest intellectuals still take seats there and browse.

Other thinkers and escapists stake out the nearby cafés, rich in Italian aromas and heady atmosphere. One further cultural note: A **plaque** set on the wall of the Condor nightspot at Broadway and Columbus claims that this is the birthplace of both topless (in 1964) and bottomless (1969) entertainment.

Russian Hill

You're unlikely to find any Russians on genteel Russian Hill, or not alive anyway. In the earliest days of San Francisco this was a burial ground for the crews of Russian trapping and fishing ships.

Bound by Francisco, Hyde, Lombard, and Taylor streets, Russian Hill is best reached by public transport, owing to driving and parking problems. Some of the streets here are so steep they simply turn into stairways. As for streets that are fit for cars – with very brave or foolhardy drivers at their wheel – have a look at Filbert Street, which is between Leavenworth and Hyde streets. The grade here is 31.5 percent, the steepest in the city, according to the municipal Bureau of Engineering. If you insist on driving along it, be sure your brakes are in top-notch condition and take the crest *very* slowly.

The "crookedest street in the world," Lombard Street is one of the prettiest, too.

Another amazing thoroughfare is the 1000 block of Lombard Street, the **"crookedest street in the world,"** between Hyde and Leavenworth. To ease the stress, eight switchbacks were installed, cutting the incline to a mere 18 percent.

Among architectural highlights, see the **Octagonal house** at 1067 Green Street, which was built before the Civil War. At the time there was a theory that eight-sided houses were better for the health than the usual quadrangular design. The only other house of this kind here, 2645 Gough Street, is

Hangers-on traveling by cable car, a system often threatened with closure.

open three afternoons per month. Check with the Colonial Dames of America, Tel: (415) 441-7512.

Cable Cars

A genuine National Landmark on the go! If you thought cable cars were just a tourist gimmick, don't mention it to the San Franciscans aboard. It's quite clearly one of the most enjoyable and exciting ways to travel, and one which you simply must experience.

Whether crammed into the passenger compartment, braving the elements on benches facing outwards, or even standing on the running board and hanging on, you could never have known that 9.5 mph (15 km/h) would feel so reckless. The crewmen are gregarious, and chat and joke with the passengers, but they are very stern about where you sit or stand; follow their orders.

The cable cars themselves are powerless. To travel, the gripman has to clamp onto the moving cable, which propels the car until he releases the grip and signals the brakeman to apply the brakes. The grip mechanism and the brakes have to be replaced quite often, and when a cable breaks everything must stop until it can be mended.

San Francisco Highlights

Two or three days is barely long enough to see the city, but if you're tight for time, here are the most popular places to spend those precious hours.

Alcatraz Island: A little bleak for young kids, but fascinating if you have an interest in prisons. The view of the city is an added bonus *(see page 38)*.

Cable Cars: A bit of history on wheels and immensely fun. Go early to avoid the lines on Powell Street or try catching a car a few stops above the turn-around *(see page 46)*.

Chinatown: A walk along crowded Stockton Street on an afternoon or weekend is literally sensational – among the outdoor vegetable markets, the smell of fish, the old women pushing past with their full shopping baskets, and the incessant traffic, you'll be awash in sights, smells, and sounds *(see page 26)*.

Fisherman's Wharf: Millions of tourists can't all be wrong, can they? Purely and simply a tourist attraction, and a fine place to pick up a sweatshirt *(see page 33)*.

Golden Gate Bridge: If you don't have the time or energy to walk across the bridge, make your way to the little park underneath *(see page 41)*.

Golden Gate Park: One of the loveliest open urban spaces in the country, providing nature walks and cultural opportunities *(see page 58)*.

Union Square: Convenient, high-ticket shopping and excellent dining in one central location *(see page 25)*.

Yerba Buena Gardens: An example of urban renewal in all its glory, including cultural pursuits, excellent family entertainment, as well as rampant consumerism *(see page 51)*.

Outrageously out of date, the cable car system has often been threatened with closure for efficiency reasons, but in 1964 the cable cars were added to the National Register of Historic Places. In the 1980s all the lines were shut down for nearly two years for top-to-bottom renovation. The ancient cars, back in action, are too close to San Francisco's heart to be endangered again for a long time.

Nob Hill

The "nob" in Nob Hill is short for "nabob," an old-fashioned English word from India for a rich and powerful man. The nabobs who settled on this smart California Street hilltop had made their fortune in the gold rush days, as often as not in the railroad business. All four rail barons – Charles Crocker, Mark Hopkins, Leland Stanford, and Collis Huntington – built private palaces here in the 1870s, as the newfangled cable car was then making the hill accessible. Three of them now have their names attached to luxury hotels on Nob Hill, the exception being Charles Crocker, whose family very generously gave their land as the site of Grace Cathedral *(see page 49)*.

Today, five-star hotels and elite apartment blocks have displaced all the old mansions, except one. Behind its brass filigreed fence, the **Pacific Union Club** at 1000 California Street was once the 42-room home of one James Flood, a saloon-keeper who became one of the kings of the Comstock Silver Lode. Although the interior of the mansion was entirely burned out in the 1906 fire, the brownstone sobriety remains intact. This traditional gentlemen's club, also known as the P-U, is the city's most exclusive. Unlike the club, the fashionable hotels of Nob Hill admit women. In fact, just about anyone can slip into the hotel lobbies or have a drink in any of the attractive bars.

Grace Cathedral, an Episcopal tribute to Gothic style, was built in 1964. Although it does resemble Notre Dame of Paris, this impressive church is built of concrete and steel – not stone – as an anti-earthquake precaution. The gilded bronze doors of the east entrance are replicas of the 15th-century *Gates of Paradise* sculpted by Lorenzo Ghiberti for the Baptistery in Florence.

MARKET STREET

Mostly as straight as an arrow, the wide diagonal of Market Street marches from the bay-front right to the edge of Twin Peaks. It starts promisingly among ambitious skyscrapers, then rambles on to the sort of neighborhood you wouldn't want to linger in.

In Huntington Park, an elegant fountain exemplifies the tone of affluent Nob Hill.

Nearest to the Embarcadero is the **Rincon Center**, a modern development of shops, offices, and apartments attached to what was originally a branch post office. The federal government sponsored the murals, depicting events from the history of San Francisco. A splendid atrium has a free-falling waterfall decorating its center.

Of all the imposing buildings along Market Street, two hotels stand out for their originality, although they couldn't be more dissimilar. The **Sheraton Palace Hotel**, at Market and New Montgomery streets, was the city's original luxury hotel, expensively redone at the end of the 1980s. Its awesome, glass-domed Garden Court is a sumptuous setting for breakfast, tea, dinner, or just a peek at how the other half lives. The contemporary **San Francisco Marriott Hotel**, at Market and Fourth, contrasts with its very daring post-modern design. Some critics think it looks like a 40-story jukebox. Love it or hate it, it's impossible to miss.

A shopping mall with a distinctive flavor is the **San Francisco Centre** (note the British spelling, which is supposed to add to the up-market feeling). It has raised the tone at Fifth and Market streets with its incredible spiral escalators, still a source of amazement for many visitors. The top five floors all belong to the Nordstrom department store.

South of Market

For some years now, South of Market Street, or **SoMa**, has been in upheaval, as gentrification razes buildings and raises rents in what had long been the dreariest of underprivileged neighborhoods – which quickly became the city's hippest enclave and the center of Internet activity. The biggest

SoMa's got the MOMA – and the Yerba Buena Gardens, too.

of the projects that has revolutionized the area is **Yerba Buena Gardens**, which includes the **Moscone Convention Center**, named after the assassinated Mayor George Moscone *(see page 22)*. It is an enormous exhibition complex, mostly underground, and big enough to hold a political convention (the Democrats staged theirs here in 1984). The lovely gardens have brought a welcome presence to the area along with enough amusements to keep visitors busy for an entire day. For youngsters, there's a carousel that originally graced the long demolished Playland at the Beach, an ice skating rink, bowling alley, and **Zeum**, a hands-on technology/arts center specifically geared to older kids and teenagers. Across Howard Street you'll no doubt be drawn toward the new **Sony Metreon**, a huge entertainment complex with 15 theaters (including an Imax), a half dozen restaurants, cutting edge technology stores, and an interactive video room, the "Airtight Garage." The games actually appeal to grownups as well as kids, unless you're sensitive to noise, of which there's a great deal.

The most prominent building nearby is the stunning **San Francisco Museum of Modern Art** (MOMA), whose works include paintings and sculptures by Matisse, Klee, Pollock, and other major artists of the modernist schools; included, too, is an extensive collection of photography. In the daytime, art lovers come here to inspect the galleries, shop in the gift store, and lunch in the café. SoMa also supports a lively nightlife venue along Folsom Street.

Tucked inside a rather nondescript building a half-block from the Metreon is the **Cartoon Art Museum** (655 Mission Street). Endowed by *Peanuts* creator Charles M. Schulz, the museum is a treasure trove of artwork and books, featuring underground and mainstream cartoonists from America and abroad. Closed Mondays, the museum charges a modest entry fee.

THE NEIGHBORHOODS

Mission District

Mission Street runs parallel to Market Street until Van Ness Avenue, where it bends into a north–south direction and becomes the main stem of the Mission District. It is an ethnically diverse area, the neighborhood of choice for Mexicans, Central and South Americans, and San Franciscans seeking somewhat affordable housing.

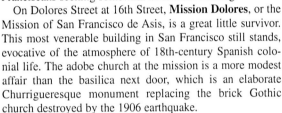

On Dolores Street at 16th Street, **Mission Dolores**, or the Mission of San Francisco de Asis, is a great little survivor. This most venerable building in San Francisco still stands, evocative of the atmosphere of 18th-century Spanish colonial life. The adobe church at the mission is a more modest affair than the basilica next door, which is an elaborate Churrigueresque monument replacing the brick Gothic church destroyed by the 1906 earthquake.

The restored ceiling of the elongated, narrow church of Mission Dolores is decorated with brightly colored Indian motifs; the carved altars came from Mexico. A small museum on the premises shows how the California missions were constructed, and there is a collection of photographs of a visit here by the Pope in the 1980s. A walled-in cemetery beside the church also serves as a botanical garden, a restful place with more than 100 varieties of flowers, most of them in bloom. A statue of the founder of the mission system, Father Junípero Serra, was the work of blind sculptor Arthur Putnam.

The merchants along **24th Street** below Dolores Street call their thoroughfare the Mission District's "Boulevard of the Americas," and a Mexican national holiday is celebrated here on 5 May *(see page 94)* with a colorful parade. There are dozens of brilliantly tinted Mexican-style murals, as well as plenty of exotic grocery stores and several restaurants offering tempting Mexican cuisine. Above Dolores Street on 24th Street is the central artery of **Noe Valley**, a neighborhood of Victorian houses, dogs, and plenty of babies in strollers and backpacks.

Civic Center

Monumental grandeur is the keynote of the San Francisco Civic Center, built after the 1906 quake with unbounded optimism and funds. The scope and size of this center of municipal government can't be matched anywhere else in the United States.

San Francisco's formidable City Hall is especially striking when lit up at night.

City Hall rather resembles the Capitol building in Washington, but the black and gold dome of the San Francisco structure (patterned on St. Peter's in Rome) is even higher. Inside the great rotunda, over the clock, is inscribed the name of James Rolph, Jr. ("Mayor 1912–1931"). Surely any first-class dictator would envy "Sunny Jim" Rolph this monument; the ceremonial staircase all but cries out for magnificent evening gowns and tails.

The **Main Public Library** occupies a new, faux-Beaux-Arts building across from its old genuine Beaux-Arts headquarters, which in 2003 reopened as the **Asian Art Museum** (hitherto in Golden Gate Park). The collection includes more than 13,000 objects from China, India, Iran, Japan, Korea, the Himalayas and Southeast Asia. **United Nations Plaza**, named after the world organization founded in San Francisco in 1945, is the scene of a farmers' market on Wednesday and Sunday.

On Van Ness Avenue, behind City Hall, an ensemble of nicely balanced buildings includes the **Opera House**, **Symphony Hall**, and the **California State Office Building**.

The Castro

This is a friendly neighborhood, well stocked with coffee shops, boutiques, and bookshops, but you'll soon notice

A streetcar takes its route through the Castro district, the cultural heart of San Francisco's gay community.

something is different. Castro Street is the main street of the district most closely associated with San Francisco's gay community – which constitutes a numerically and politically significant proportion of the city's population. The biggest annual parade in San Francisco is the Lesbian/Gay Pride Celebration in June, which involves the participation of hundreds of thousands of people of many orientations.

When the Muni Metro train stops at Castro Street station, you surface in **Harvey Milk Plaza**, which is named after the first avowedly gay member of the city board of supervisors. He was martyred in the City Hall assassination of 1977. The wittily named specialized shops of Castro Street are the most unusual monuments, except for the classic 1920s cinema palace, the **Castro Theatre**, in Art Deco style. At 1800 Market Street, the **San Francisco Lesbian, Gay, Bisexual and Transgender Community Center** promotes a dynamic range of activities that support the community.

Up the hill from here, **Twin Peaks** are not quite the tallest hills in town, but nearly. The lucky folk whose houses are perched on the hillsides enjoy unparalleled views of the San Francisco skyline and the bay.

Japantown

A modern interpretation of a five-tiered round pagoda towers above Japantown, or Nihonmachi (between Geary, Webster, California and Octavia streets), where the city's sizeable Japanese population comes to stock up on ethnic food, books, and films. The **Peace Pagoda**, a gift from the people of Japan, is surmounted by a graceful nine-ringed spire symbolizing the highest virtue and supporting a golden sphere with a flaming head.

Japanese people have lived in San Francisco since the 1860s. The darkest era was World War II, when Japanese-Americans

The Peace Pagoda – a gift from Japan – towers high above Japantown.

were sent to internment camps *(see page 21)*. After the war, many returned, however, and during the 1960s the Japan Center transformed the area into a commercial zone with air-conditioned shopping malls, offices, sushi bars, restaurants, and a hotel and spa. Bibliophiles will enjoy browsing in the Kinokuniya bookstore, an enormous bookshop specializing in books and magazines about Japan.

Just east of Japantown, at Gough and Geary streets, **St. Mary's Cathedral** is the city's most unusual religious structure, replacing a smaller Catholic cathedral destroyed by fire in 1962. Its modern architecture zooms heavenward. American and Italian architects and engineers joined forces in geometric experiments – the cupola is described as a hyperbolic parabola, with a volume of nearly 2,135,000 cubic ft (60,000 cubic m). The ingredients combine in a harmonious whole, with red-brick floors, wood, glass, reinforced concrete, and marble. Covering two city blocks, the cathedral can accommodate 2,400 worshippers, seated on three sides of the altar. The modern organ, built in Padua, Italy, counterpoints the architectural innovations; it has 4,842 pipes.

Pacific Heights

For mansion-watchers, rubber-necking in the Pacific Heights district is more gratifying than in Nob Hill. There's an extra-ordinary collection of dream houses along Broadway and Vallejo streets built by wealth and well endowed with good taste. Architectural features, down to the window shutters and doorknobs, are as original as the flowerbeds and the shrubbery. Many of the fine Edwardian and Victorian homes have remained in private hands, while others function as schools, museums, or consulates.

One of the advantages of living in Pacific Heights is the ready availability of wide-open spaces for walking the dog, playing tennis, or gazing at the skyline. Covering four blocks with trees, flowers, and grass, **Lafayette Park** is the highest of the area's hilltop parks. Another treat afforded by this charmed summit is a superior view of Alcatraz *(see page 38)* – just behind the **Spreckels Mansion**, built by one of the sugar barons and currently owned by the novelist Danielle Steele. Modesty has never entered the picture here, and the house might be mistaken as an impressive neo-classical bank or opera house.

Another mansion full of character is the **Haas-Lilienthal House** at 2007 Franklin Street, dating from 1886. Its design is a conglomeration of geometrical shapes – triangles, cones, cubes, and cylinders. Although it is now occupied by the Foundation for San Francisco's Architectural Heritage, you can rent the ballroom for private special events.

Alta Plaza is another Pacific Heights hilltop park of note, steeply terraced and with fine views.

Due south, in the Western Addition, keen photographers head for **Alamo Square** for the picture-perfect row of admirably filigreed Victorian houses in the foreground, with the skyscraper skyline and the bay behind.

Haight-Ashbury

The golden age of Haight-Ashbury is long over, but the reputation and the smell of incense lingers on. You'll notice among the passers-by that there's a high percentage of people on another wavelength and way too many panhandling teenagers. Fond memories of Flower Power and the Summer of Love are recalled in the esoteric shops.

Rebels with flowers in their hair took over the district in the 1960s, pursuing noble goals and, on a more individual level, comprehensive hedonism. The world's infatuation with "Hashbury" and its ideals soon cooled, however, and now nostalgia has taken over. Middle-aged ex-hippies, along with children of the "flower children," can be seen window-shopping along **Haight Street**, looking out for handmade sandals, second-hand clothes, psychedelic art, ancient gramophone records, alternative lifestyle books, and organic food.

 ## Golden Gate Park

One of the largest man-made parks in the world unfolds right from the edge of Haight-Ashbury to the Pacific Ocean.

Out of the Dunes

They laughed in 1870 when civil engineer William H. Hall said San Francisco's barren "Outside Lands" could be reclaimed and turned into a botanical celebration. His hand-picked successor, Scottish-born John McLaren, was determined to finish the job — and he was still at it when he died at the age of 93.

Golden Gate Park, a vast green monument to the two dreamers, is filled with anglers, archers, baseball players, cyclists, and enthusiasts of sports, nature, and culture. Parking can be difficult, but there's still room for everyone.

Golden Gate Park is by any standard a triumph of landscaping. Drifting dunes have been transformed into an oasis covered with trees and shrubs of every shade of green, flowers that always seem to be in bloom, and lawns that make you want to run barefoot over them. Recreational activities to suit a wide range of ages and tastes are sprinkled liberally across the park's 1,017 acres (412 hectares), along with several first-class cultural attractions.

The **Conservatory of Flowers**, the oldest building in the park, was badly damaged in a storm a few years back and has yet to be repaired. Money is still being

Beautifully restored homes line Alamo Square, framed by the city skyline.

raised to bring this copy of the famous Palm House in London's Kew Gardens back to its former glory.

One of San Francisco's primary art museums, the **M.H. de Young Memorial Museum**, has been forced to close temporarily as a result of seismic instability. A new building is being constructed in the same location, and the museum is scheduled to reopen in spring 2005. The collection includes art ranging from colonial to contemporary times, as well as landscapes and sculptures from the American West and a range of textiles and furniture.

With its manicured shrubs and koi pond, the Japanese Tea Garden is a favorite stop for visitors at Golden Gate Park.

The Asian Art Museum that was next door has now moved to the Civic Center *(see page 54)*.

The **California Academy of Sciences**, on the opposite side of the Music Concourse, has something for everyone: live crocodiles, a stuffed grizzly bear, and a merry-go-round for giant fish. If you thought science was too serious, attend an informal talk by a real scientist, or wander into the exhibit of original "Far Side" cartoons by Gary Larson.

Tour buses park near the **Japanese Tea Garden**, a favorite stop on their routes. All the requisite Japanese subtleties are represented here, from rocks among carefully tended shrubs to a koi pond and bridge. Other treasures include a bronze Buddha from Tajima, Japan, a zen garden, a *tsukubai*, an ornamental water basin and a 60-ft (18-meter) tall Buddhist pagoda.

The Richmond and Sunset

Set on a dramatic promontory overlooking **Seal Rocks**, the haunt of throngs of sea lions and sea-birds, Cliff House is now a bar and restaurant for tourists, with a fine view and mediocre food. Below is a visitor center, the **Musée Mécanique** (though in September 2002 this moved temporarily to Pier 45 at the foot of Taylor Street in Fisherman's Wharf while Cliff House was renovated) housing dozens of historic relics of penny arcades, and a Camera Obscura, projecting a "live" panorama into a dark room – as eerie an experience today as it was when Leonardo da Vinci got the idea back in the 15th century. Across the road, the eucalyptus, cypress, and pine forests of **Sutro Heights Park** were planted by Adolph Sutro, a German immigrant who became the mayor of San Francisco.

Ocean Beach offers about 4 miles (6 km) of inviting sand. Swimming is permitted though many people opt for wetsuits since the water is extremely cold. Even wading here is dangerous because of the undertow, but sunbathing and sunset watching remain appealing.

On the landward side of the Great Highway, parallel to Ocean Beach, **San Francisco Zoo**, one of the country's older municipal animal parks, has recently undergone renovation and expansion. It's easy to reach by public transport – at the end of the Muni "L Taraval" streetcar line. Among the novelties you'll see snow leopards, penguins, and koalas from Australia.

EXCURSIONS

Within day-trip distance of San Francisco you can experience the most varied scenery and attractions: picturesque harbors, inspiring forests, crashing surf, vineyards as far as the eye can see, and enviable college towns.

When is a day trip too grueling? San Francisco excursion companies advertise one-day return tours that go as far as Yosemite National Park – more than 16 hours from start to finish. Lake Tahoe is slightly closer. If you are driving, the wine country north of San Francisco makes a relatively easy day trip, although you may enjoy it more if you take it at a leisurely pace, staying at least one night in a country inn for relaxed wine tasting and gourmet dining.

Here are some ideas for feasible excursions, organized or improvised. We start in the East Bay, move to Marin County, visit Wine Country, and then travel southward to South San Francisco and Monterey.

East Bay

Oakland

If Oakland were just a few hours north from its actual location, it would be a major attraction. But as it stands, in the overwhelming shadow of San Francisco (that sensational skyline is visible from the Oakland waterfront), it's only a sideshow. How cruel of Gertrude Stein to have written of Oakland, "There is no there there." The city is worth your while, though, and it gives you an excuse to ride the comfortable, fast BART (Bay Area Rapid Transit) line beneath the bay – among the supreme American achievements in public transport. Alternatively, you can drive over the Bay Bridge.

The BART train deposits you in the City Square shopping zone, with post-modern skyscrapers in view – though Oakland is not really a skyscraper metropolis. The second impression may cool the initial euphoria; Oakland is a big industrial port city with a few enclaves of glamor, including about 60,000 acres (25,000 hectares) of parklands. With a population of nearly 400,000, Oakland shows a rare ethnic fabric. The census counts just under half the inhabitants as African-American, 34 percent Caucasian, 9 percent Hispanic, and 8 percent Asian and Pacific islanders. All this explains the city's cosmopolitan shopping and eating possibilities.

Oakland takes a breather, however, in wide open spaces at the heart of the city. **Lake Merritt**, a 155-acre (63-hectare) salt-water lake, has been a game refuge since 1870. It is surrounded by gardens, recreational facilities, and colorful modern apartment and office buildings.

Near the south shore of the lake, the low-lying **Oakland Museum** is subtitled the Museum of California. The contents are top-rate, the displays imaginative and the lushly landscaped architecture exciting. The history department, on the second level, has engrossing exhibits on subjects as old as prehistoric inscriptions and as recent as the beatnik era and beyond. Here you'll find all you need to know about the California dream—how it was born and evolved, from the Spanish conquistadores to gold miners to Hollywood hopefuls. The **Gallery of California Art**, on the third level, displays over 550 revealing works. Starting with the gold rush, newly arrived artists were fascinated by the California sunshine, the people of several races, the drama of Yosemite, and San Francisco Bay. (The museum is closed on Monday, Tuesday, and principal holidays.)

Finally, **Jack London Square**, named in honor of the author who grew up in Oakland, is a shopping, eating, and strolling complex on the shore of the estuary. The seafood restaurants enjoy appetizing views of the busy bay and the San Francisco skyline. For historical interest, a primitive cabin on show here is identified as the one Jack London lived in when he followed the gold rush to the Yukon. Heinhold's First and Last Chance Saloon, a few steps away, is said to have been a

London haunt. Just in case you think you've had too much to drink, it's the bar that's tilting; it was salvaged from an old whaler. A floating historic monument is the restored yacht **Potomac**, moored along here, which served as President Franklin Roosevelt's official pleasure craft. After Roosevelt's death, the yacht suffered its ups and downs – Elvis Presley once owned it, and it later sank at Treasure Island.

Berkeley

For a bird's-eye view of the city skyline and the bay check out Campanile Tower in Berkeley.

The brainiest place in the West is the University of California at Berkeley. If a bright idea really did glow like the light bulb in comic strips, this campus would look like the Great White Way. With more than 30,000 top-flight students and a faculty that includes a galaxy of Nobel prize-winners, Berkeley can permit itself a swagger of pride and a jot of eccentricity.

Interest in the Athens of the Pacific focuses not on the city of Berkeley (notable for its bookstores and gourmet restaurants), but on the campus within, a spacious monument to California's endeavor for academic excellence. Start at the **Student Union** building, where a visitor center supplies maps and information. They also offer guided tours of the campus, but you don't really have to wander far from the

Union to get the feeling of student life, with all its passions and fashions.

For a global vantage point, take the elevator (for a small charge) up **Sather Tower**, otherwise known as the Campanile, which has a 12-bell carillon. It is 307 ft (94 m) tall and modeled on the one in the Piazza San Marco in Venice. From the top the view puts the town and campus into perspective and offers a superb bird's-eye view of San Francisco, the skyline, and the bay.

Just west of the Campanile, the **Bancroft Library** has exhibits of rare books and manuscripts as well as what's billed as the actual nugget that set off the gold rush.

Stadium Rim Road leads to Strawberry Canyon, where you can enjoy roaming the restful yet scientifically significant **Botanical Gardens**. Beyond, the **Lawrence Hall of Science** honors Ernest Lawrence, the first Berkeley professor to win the Nobel Prize (in 1939) and the developer of the cyclotron. The building is more than a physics laboratory; it's a sort of hands-on science fair for children and adults who want to come to grips with the long and the short of science, from astronomy to biology. (Admission is charged.)

The **Hearst Museum of Anthropology** in Kroeber Hall has unusual exhibits on the cultures of several continents. Closer to home, there are artifacts from the last California Indian tribesman to come into contact with modern society – Ishi – who eluded the white man until 1911, when he came in from the wild.

Across Bancroft Way, the **University Art Museum** has been described as an interpretation of New York's coiled Guggenheim – with corners. Angular spiral ramps are tilted to supersede stairs in a stark concrete interior, which is used to host traveling exhibitions. There are 11 galleries and a sculpture garden.

Observe Mother Nature at her finest – whale-watching from atop Point Reyes Lighthouse.

Telegraph Avenue is a landmark of the counter-culture. Here the rebellious children of the protest generation dress more or less as their peacenik parents when Berkeley spawned the radical student movement that swept through the United States in the 1960s, struggling for free speech and against the Vietnam War.

Squatting on the sidewalks, young people today meditate, sell trinkets, tell your fortune, or hand out leaflets about causes they consider just as urgent as their ancestors' crusades. This is still the perfect place to organize an insurrection.

Marin County

You can also take an even bigger boat, a public ferry, from San Francisco to Sausalito, a half-hour trip. If you drive across the Golden Gate Bridge instead, the views are thrilling, but parking in Sausalito verges on the impossible.

During World War II Sausalito prospered, producing Liberty ships on an assembly line. Now one of these abandoned industrial structures houses the San Francisco Bay-Delta Tidal Hydraulic Model, **Bay Model** for short. Covering 1 acre (0.4 hectares), the computerized model simulates the tides. The US Army Corps of Engineers runs tours.

Tiburon, a pleasant harbor town that can be reached by ferryboat, capitalizes on its wonderful views of the San Francisco skyline. In the foreground is **Angel Island**, long used for military purposes but now a state park. At Tiburon's ferry slip is Main Street, a little shopping artery full of character. Follow it around the bend to Ark Row, where you can see pretty houseboats which have been beached and converted into shops.

One of California's most distinguished buildings is visible from Highway 101 north of San Rafael. The blue-domed **Marin County Civic Center**, a vast hilltop project, was the last work designed by Frank Lloyd Wright. This brilliantly landscaped experiment houses all manner of facilities, from theaters and the county library to the hall of justice.

If you have time for only one brief whiff of California wilderness, try to make it **Muir Woods National Monument**, a mere 12 miles (19 km) north of the Golden Gate Bridge. The park's 6 miles (10 km) of nature trails offer a sense of tranquillity in the shade of the timeless Coast Redwood trees *(Sequoia sempervirens)*. The aroma of the forest stimulates the lungs and the spirit. The trees –the oldest of which is a thousand years old—are 250 ft (76 m) tall and 14 ft (4 m) thick. The furrows in their bark, like the wrinkles in an old face, seem to attest to all they have survived. The woods are named in honor of the Scottish-born conservationist John Muir (1838–1914).

Another gorgeous spot is the **Point Reyes National Seashore**. The coastline here is so rugged and the surf is so violent that the leaflet and map available at the Bear Valley Visitor Center is full of warnings such as "Don't go near the water" and "No life guard on duty." From December to April, whale-watchers mount the observation platform of the **Point Reyes Lighthouse**, which overlooks a notorious graveyard for ships. The famous San Andreas Fault, source of all those earthquakes, separates this peninsula from the mainland, and you can visit the **Earthquake Trail**, near the Visitor Center, which points out traces of the 1906 disaster.

Wine Country

The most crowded time to visit the vineyards north of San Francisco is during the grape harvest, in September or October. All year round, however, the beauty of this region is striking, the eating, drinking, and shopping are enjoyable, and the wine tasting is superb. Serious wine buffs will find literature at local tourist offices, in bookshops, and at the wineries, but here is a glance at what's in store, and where.

 Napa Valley

The scenery of America's most famous wine-growing region, Napa County looks like Spain at its most beautiful – rolling

hills of grapevines and grazing land, eucalyptus, haughty palms and cedars, and flowers alongside the road. You can tour Napa Valley by coach, car, or bicycle, by luxurious vintage train, or from the perspective of a glider or hot-air balloon.

The valley begins at the town of **Napa**, with a population of more than 65,000. A neat and pleasant county

Muir Woods – tranquillity, open air, and timeless shade – an elixir for the spirit.

seat with an ably staffed visitors' center in the central pedestrian area, this is the place to check in for maps, leaflets, and suggestions on accommodation, eating, and wine tasting. In the summer and on weekends, the hotels fill quickly as do the more popular restaurants, so advanced reservations are a good idea.

Northward, the small town of **Yountville** moved into big-time tourism when its giant old winery and distillery were converted into a shopping-and-eating complex, Vintage 1870. Among the nearby wineries are the French-run Domaine Chandon, for sparkling wine; Robert Mondavi, the last word in computerized wine making; and Inglenook-Napa Valley, with tastings in the hundred-year-old heart of the modern operation. Farther afield you'll find the Hess Collection, a Swiss art lover's contemporary museum and winery.

St Helena is a delightful small town which was smart enough to resist "progress"—at least on the 1890s-style

Let There Be Wine

The Spanish padres who founded missions throughout California were the first to grow grapes here; they needed wine, if only for sacramental purposes. But serious commercial production began in the Sonoma Valley in 1857, thanks to a colorful, wine-loving Hungarian nobleman.

With many varieties of cuttings he imported from Europe, Count Agoston Haraszthy established the Buena Vista Winery, which is still in operation. He also founded something of an international dynasty. The count's two sons, niftily named Arpad and Attila, married the daughters of the region's Mexican commander, General Mariano Guadalupe Vallejo, simultaneously, at the Sonoma Mission. Count Haraszthy eventually vanished in Nicaragua.

main street (the local ironmonger does go in for antiques these days). Just north of town you'll find Beringer Vineyards, founded in 1876, and Christian Brothers, where the monks' traditions are still followed in a stone winery.

Since the mid-19th century **Calistoga** has been somewhere for "taking the waters" – and subsequently the wines as well. California's first millionaire, publisher and banker Sam Brannan, bought the land and capitalized on the natural springs. He had planned to name the place Saratoga, after a fashionable spa back east, but during a drinking bout he announced, "We'll make this place the Calistoga of Sarafornia." He died in poverty, but Calistoga flourishes with its volcanic ash mud baths and rejuvenation facilities. When it comes out of the ground the magic water is boiling hot, but it's also bottled and drunk cold – and sold almost everywhere here.

Among the nearby wineries, the most unconventional is Clos Pegase, which combines startling post-modern architecture, an art collection, and stylish wines. Like much of the Napa Valley, it's aimed at the trendy up-market set.

Closer than Yellowstone National Park, you can see a real Old Faithful Geyser just a few miles north of Calistoga. The 60-ft (18-m) jet of boiling water and vapor shoots out of the ground every 50 minutes. Admission is charged.

☞ Sonoma Valley

Closer to San Francisco than the Napa Valley, and more relaxed about entertaining city slickers, the Sonoma Valley offers generous helpings of history along with fine wine.

Sonoma, a captivating town and the county seat, is just how American small towns used to look, with everyone congregating for a chat in the shade of the main square, diagonal parking along its side, and chickens marching about the

Fine wine, sumptuous food, great shops, and balmy year-round weather – if it's not heaven, it must be Napa Valley.

lawn. Much aware of its charms, Sonoma nevertheless manages to maintain its modesty.

The main square, **Sonoma Plaza**, covers 8 acres (3 hectares) – vast even by California standards. It contains the city hall, the tourist office, and a duck pond. History was made here in 1846, as a monument in the square recounts, when the flag of the California Republic was first raised. This was a grass-roots American revolt against Mexican rule, which was overtaken by events less than a month later. The Bear Flag is now the official flag of the state of California.

Northeast of the plaza, the San Francisco **Solano Mission**, founded in 1823, is the northernmost of the 21 California missions. The paintings in the adobe church were done by Indian parishioners.

Other buildings around the square include a Mexican army barracks, 19th-century hotels, and historic homes which are now shops and restaurants. Nearby is the house built by General Vallejo, American-Victorian-Gingerbread in style, and quite possibly the most un-Mexican house in the whole of California. He called it "Lachryma Montis," the Latin translation of the original Indian name for this area–"crying mountain."

The wine trail starts within the Sonoma city limits. The Sebastiani Vineyards, producing everything from serious vintages to jugs of popular wines, has tours and tastings. Just outside town is Buena Vista, which maintains a tasting room at 18000 Old Winery Road. Ravenswood, known for producing "big reds" like Zinfandel, at 18701 Gehricke Road, offers tours, tastings, and barbecues. Quirky Gundlach Bundschu winery is a fun place to visit and known for world class cabernet wines.

Farther on is the Beauty Ranch, now the **Jack London State Historic Park**, a memorial to the best-selling author of *Call of the Wild* and *The Sea Wolf*. The House of Happy Walls, now a museum, was built by London's widow after he died in 1916. On display are souvenirs he picked up while in the South Pacific, his typewriters and eyeshades, and even his first rejection slips. Literary pilgrims from many countries come to see the museum, and hike to London's grave on a nearby hill.

South of San Francisco

Two main highways run southeastward down the San Francisco peninsula. By the bay, Interstate 101, linking the city with the airport, can be as jammed and intimidating as one of the Los Angeles freeways. Somewhat less stressful, and definately more picturesque, is the inland route,

Interstate highway 280 (or the Junípero Serra Freeway), with a scenery bonus of dramatic mountainous countryside.

Just by the Edgewood Road exit of I-280, you can visit the stately home of **Filoli**, with 16 acres (6.5 hectares) of formal gardens – as seen on the television series *Dynasty*. "Filoli" may sound Italian, but it's an acronym for Fight, Love, Live. It was the motto of the owner of the estate, William Bourn, who inherited a gold-rush fortune and parlayed it to even greater wealth as owner of San Francisco's water supply and the head of the gas company. The gardens, improved over more than half a century, have something in bloom most of the year. Tours are operated from Tuesday to Saturday, mostly between February and November. To obtain admission details and make reservations, Tel: (650) 364-2880.

Sonoma Valley combines small town America with the historic west, local shops, and lush vineyards, for genuine family fun.

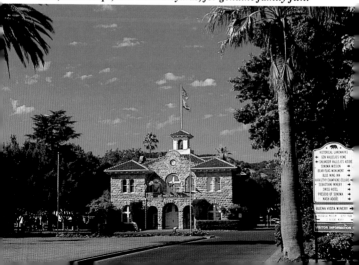

Palo Alto looks like everybody's idea of a small city in contemporary America, a model that is not often seen outside the movies. In the real world of traffic jams, junk-food joints, and litter, it's hard to match the tranquil tree-shaded charm and easy-going pace of University Avenue and the intersecting streets. Palo Alto is a college town, home of a rich, famous, and academically distinguished private university.

Founded in 1885 by the railroad tycoon Leland Stanford, **Stanford University** occupies a dream campus so vast you need a bus, a bike, or a car to get around. It covers 8,180 acres (3,310 hectares) from the Santa Clara Valley to the foothills of the Santa Cruz Mountains. An avenue of stately palms leads from town to the center of campus, the cloistered Main Quadrangle, whose architecture is described as a mixture of Romanesque and Mission Revival.

The tallest and most striking building on campus, the **Hoover Tower**, honors an alumnus, US President Herbert Hoover. The tower and neighboring buildings house the Hoover Institution on War, Revolution and Peace, where great political thinkers have researched and deliberated both during and after the Cold War. From the top of the tower (admission charged) you can see the expanse of Mediterranean-style tile roofs that begins on campus and stretches out as far as the sea.

Admirers of beautiful college campuses should continue from Silicon Valley to **Santa Cruz**, where a redwood forest hides the Santa Cruz division of the state-run University of California system. For its landscape and modern architecture, UCSC, which opened in 1966, is a dynamic endeavor. But there's more than intellectual activity hereabouts. The city of Santa Cruz itself, down the hill, has a 1-mile- (1.6-km-) long swimming beach and an old-fashioned boardwalk with vintage amusement park.

☞ Monterey Peninsula

A scenic three-hour drive south of San Francisco brings you to the Monterey Peninsula, a happy convergence of history, charm, and some of the world's most astounding seascapes. Thanks to the work of conservationists, lobbyists, and far-sighted politicians, the sea lions and seabirds enjoy an unthreatened life along the cliffs and beaches, cypress forests thrive on the ocean breezes, and the towns remain eminently desirable. Despite several million tourists who swoop in every year, high standards are maintained.

The peninsula's principal city, **Monterey**, was the capital of Spanish, Mexican, and briefly, American California, until the gold rush shifted attention to Sacramento. The hilltop **Presidio** of Monterey, the first of the Spanish fortresses founded in California, serves to this day as a

With its long beach, old-fashioned boardwalk, and vintage amusement park, Santa Cruz is a great place to visit.

United States Army base – the home of the Defense Language Institute, where military interpreters are trained. Also in Monterey is another elite military institution, the US Naval Postgraduate School.

Crowds of vacationers spend time on **Fisherman's Wharf**, with its cheery boardwalk atmosphere, seafood restaurants, and souvenir shops. Bay sightseeing boats, whale-watching tours (from mid-December until March), and deep-sea fishing expeditions all leave from here. Note the adobe **Custom House**, built in 1814. It was here that the American flag was first raised in California, in 1846.

Legend leads most visitors to Monterey's **Cannery Row**, immortalized by John Steinbeck in his 1945 novel of the same name. However, it has all been spruced up and rather fictionalized since those noisy, smelly, eccentric days. The

With breathtaking seascapes, plentiful wildlife, shops, and more – there's a million reasons to make Monterey a must.

derelict sardine canneries and related structures have been regenerated for the tourism business, and are now art galleries, shopping malls, amusements, and even a wax museum featuring characters from Steinbeck's novels.

The top tourist attraction in town is the **Monterey Bay Aquarium**. Many millions of dollars and all the best ideas in aquarium design and presentation were channeled into this institution, which was inaugurated in 1984. There are light-hearted explanations of all the phenomena of the sea, which mainly focus on the rich local scene. Monterey Canyon, just offshore, is the undersea equivalent of Arizona's Grand Canyon – it's nearly 2 miles (3 km) deep! Children of all ages will enjoy the "touching pool," which includes bat rays, a type of sting ray (but they don't sting). Meanwhile, delightful sea otters frolic both inside and outside the aquarium.

The little-frequented town of **Pacific Grove**, founded by Methodists in 1875, has an incomparable collection of Victorian cottages and a very beautiful public golf course. In addition, gulls, pelicans, cormorants, and other sea-birds in transit haunt the lovely coastline, and millions of Monarch butterflies winter here.

Seventeen-Mile Drive is so spectacular that people pay to see what lies beyond the toll booth. This is also California's golf capital, home of the exclusive Pebble Beach course.

Luxury typifies the small town of **Carmel-by-the-Sea**, the stomping ground of some well-to-do Bohemians. Here you'll find a tremendous range of art galleries, boutiques, and fashionable restaurants. At the end of the main street's incline, a seemingly endless beach of white sand begins. Carmel's 18th-century mission was the favorite of the mission system's founder, Father Junípero Serra, who is buried here.

Museums

Asian Art Museum. Golden Gate Park (though moving to Civic Center in January 2003); Tel: (415) 379-8801. Tues–Sun 9:30am–5pm; adults $7, seniors $5, children 12–17 $4, under 12 free. Admission includes same-day entry to the de Young museum.

California Academy of Sciences. Golden Gate Park; Tel: (415) 750-7145. Daily 9am–6pm Memorial Day–Labor Day; 10am–5pm Labor Day–Memorial Day; adults $8.50, seniors/students 12–17 $5.50, children 4–11 $2, under 4 free. Free the first Wednesday of the month.

California Palace of the Legion of Honor. Lincoln Park; Tel: (415) 750-3600; <www.thinker.org>. Tues–Sun 9:30am–5pm; adults $8, seniors over 65 $6, children 12–17 $5, under 12 free. Admission is free the second Wednesday of each month.

Chinese Historical Society. 965 Clay Street; Tel: (415) 391-1188. Tues–Fri 11am–4pm, Sat–Sun noon–4pm; adults $3, students and seniors $2, free first Thursday of the month.

Exploratorium. Bay and Lyon streets; Tel: (415) 561-0360; <www.exploratorium.edu>. Daily 10am–6pm summer; closed on Mondays during the school year; adults $10, seniors over 65 $7, children 6–17 $5, 3–5 $2.50, free first Wednesday in the month.

The Magnes Museum/Jewish Museum San Francisco. 121 Steuart Street; Tel: (415) 591-8800; call for exhibitions; <www.magnesmuseum.org>. Sun–Wed noon–5pm, Thurs 2–7pm. Adults $4, students and seniors $3, children under 12 free.

San Francisco Museum of Modern Art. 151 Third Street; Tel: (415) 357-4000; <www.sfmoma.org>. Thurs 11am–9pm, Fri–Tues 11am–6pm, closed Weds and major holidays; adults $10, seniors $7, students, children under 12 free; free admission on the first Tuesday of each month and half price Thursday evenings 6–9pm.

San Francisco Maritime National Historic Park. Foot of Polk Street; Tel: (415) 561-7100; <www.nps.gov/safr>. Daily 10am–5pm; free.

Wells Fargo History Museum. 420 Montgomery Street; Tel: (415) 396-2619; <www.wellsfargohistory.com/museums>. Mon–Fri 9am–5pm; free.

Attractions

Alcatraz Island. Pier 41 (Fisherman's Wharf); Tel: information: (415) 773-1188, tickets: (415) 705-5555. Times and ticket prices vary. Visit the website <www.blueandgoldfleet.com> or call.

Coit Tower. Atop Telegraph Hill; Tel: (415) 362-0808. Daily 10am–6pm; admission to the top of the tower: adults $3.75, seniors $2.50, children 6–12 $1.50.

Hyde Street Pier. Foot of Hyde Street at Beach Street; Tel: (415) 556-3002; <www.nps.gov/safr>. Daily 9.30am–5pm; adults $5, under 17 free.

Haas-Lilienthal House. 2007 Franklin Street; Tel: (415) 441-3004; <www.sfheritage.org/house.html>. One-hour tours are given Wednesdays from noon to 3pm and Sundays from 11am–4pm; adults $5, seniors 65 and over and children under 12 $3.

Lombard Street. Lombard between Hyde and Leavenworth streets. This residential street is bordered by gardens and the sidewalk is graded to make it easier for walkers.

Mission Dolores. 16th and Dolores streets; Tel: (415) 621-8203. Daily 9am–4pm; adults $3, children $2.

San Francisco Zoo, Sloat Blvd. and 45th Avenue; Tel: (415) 753-7080; <www.sfzoo.org>. Daily 10am–5pm; adults $10, seniors and children 12–17 $7, children 3–11 $4. Free the first Wednesday of month.

WHAT TO DO

ENTERTAINMENT

From grand opera and avant-garde theater to seedy strip shows, clangorous alternative music clubs, or languorous cocktail lounges, every aspect of entertainment is available in San Francisco, a noted good-time town. Particular kinds of entertainments seem to cluster in neighborhoods: Try Nob Hill for a sentimental piano bar, North Beach for the blues or jazz, Union Square for theater, Civic Center for culture. In addition, you will find congenial haunts with singular ethnic, musical, or social orientation spread all over town.

For a preview of coming attractions, turn to the Internet if handy, and investigate the excellent newspaper web sites, such as <www.sfgate.com/eguide>, <www.sfweekly.com>, <www.sfstation.com>, <www.sfbg.com>, or the city guide <bayarea.citysearch.com>. Once in town, consult the encyclopedic survey of what's on in the "Datebook" section of the whopping Sunday edition of either or the *San Francisco Chronicle* or study a copy of either *SF Weekly* or the *Bay Guardian*, a giveaway weekly easily found in bookstores, cafés, and in sidewalk kiosks.

If too much pre-planning removes all the excitement of an evening out, meander down to the TIX counter (Tel: 433-7827) on the east side of Union Square. Here, tickets for certain shows are available at half price, starting at noon on the day of the performance only. (TIX also sells full-price tickets for future performances. It's closed Sunday and Monday.)

Opera, ballet, classical music: War Memorial Opera House (Van Ness Avenue at Grove Street), in the shadow of City Hall, is one of the most glamorous venues for an evening out. The gala season of the San Francisco Opera company (Tel: 415-864-3330) runs from September to December, followed by a season of the San Francisco Ballet (Tel. 415-865-2000) on the same stage from February until June (the exact dates of these seasons vary slightly each year, so check in advance). Elsewhere, many ethnic and experimental dance companies perform at almost any time of year.

Across the street from the Opera House is the Louise M. Davies Symphony Hall, where the San Francisco Symphony Orchestra (Tel: 415-864-6000) holds forth between September and July.

Fisherman's Wharf is a stage for countless local artists and performers.

The interior design is elegant, but the acoustics controversial.

For less formal concerts, enjoy chamber music, piano and violin duos, or classically trained singers at Old First Presbyterian Church on Sacramento Street at Van Ness Avenue (Tel: 415-474-1608). Tickets are modestly priced and the cable car will take you to within two blocks of the church. Over the summer, a great variety of music is available free on Sunday afternoons at Stern Grove, in the woods at Sloat Boulevard and 19th Avenue. In the heart of North Beach, the venerable Washington Square Bar and Grill showcases jazz musicians seven nights a week (1707 Powell Street; Tel: 415 982-8123; no cover charge.)

Theater and cinema: Among dozens of theater groups, the American Conservatory Theater (415 Geary Street, Tel: 415-749-2228) has acquired the widest national reputation. Its repertory season runs from October until June. Broadway hits appear next door at the Curran Theater or, a few blocks away, the Golden Gate Theater and Orpheum. All three venues share the same telephone number (Tel: 415-551-2000). In summer there's free Shakespeare in Golden Gate Park.

As far as the cinema is concerned, first-run movies, art house cinema, and classics are shown all over the city, especially in

multiplexes along Van Ness Avenue, in Japantown, at the Embarcadero Center, and south of Market in the Metreon. The Roxie in the Mission district and the Red Vic Movie House in the Haight are two popular art-house movie theaters. The Castro Theater, an art deco movie palace built in the 1920s on Castro Street, is often the spot for interesting documentaries and film festival favorites.

Swinging in Ghirardelli Square, with its live music, shops and galleries.

Pop and rock: Venues all over town cover the musical spectrum with performances of rock, jazz, blues, and funk. The SoMa District is also a hotbed of alternative music, but the scene stretches from Union Square to Fisherman's Wharf. If you want salsa or other Latin rhythms, visit Mission District clubs such as Roccapulco (Tel: 415-648-6611).

Jazz: When big jazz names visit the area they tend to perform across the bay at Yoshi's in Oakland (Tel: 510-238-9200). In North Beach, Jazz at Pearl's (Tel: 415-291-8255) features a Monday Big Band night and local musicians Tuesday–Saturday.

Comedy and cabaret: San Francisco has a big sense of humor, and local comedy clubs have hatched the talents of many well-known personalities, including Whoopi Goldberg and Robin Williams. Cobb's Comedy Club at the Cannery (Tel: 415-928-4320) holds a Monday night showcase and regular shows the rest of the week. The Punchline (444 Battery Street; Tel: 415-397-7573) hosts nationally known and local talent nightly except Mondays. On the cabaret front, the Plush Room (940 Sutter Street; Tel: 415-885-2800) is the preferred stage for torch singers. In North Beach a gloriously silly satirical musical review, *Beach Blanket Babylon*, has been packing them in for over two decades; adults only except for Sunday matinees. Call far ahead for tickets to these immensely popular shows; Tel: (415) 421-4222.

SHOPPING

Like the city itself, shopping in San Francisco is stylish, cosmopolitan, and innovative. Here you will find whatever you've been looking for, including fashions, fads, and gadgets you never knew you needed.

Don't limit yourself to department stores or malls, where the retailers all look alike. San Francisco is full of old-fashioned neighborhoods where gourmet food markets vie for attention with ultra-cool clothing boutiques, gift shops, and bookstores. While an influx of chain stores has diminished the local color of shopping blocks here and there, every neighborhood has a number of unique stores that reflect the taste and passions of their owners.

When to Shop

Hours tend to vary from shop to shop and district to district, but the department stores operate from 9.30 or 10am to 8pm Monday–Friday, until 6 or 7pm Saturday, and from noon to 6pm on Sunday. Note that a number of smaller shops close on Sunday.

Where to Shop

The place to start for a survey of San Francisco shopping is **Union Square**, which manages to pack in more exclusive retailing than almost any other area. The nationally famous department stores are here, along with elegant boutiques down the nearby lanes. Also downtown is the **San Francisco Shopping Centre**, at Market and Fifth streets, a 9-story vertical shopping mall.

SoMa (South of Market), especially techno-savvy South Park between 2nd and 4th, Bryant, and Brannan Streets, holds treasures in fashion and home decor. Discount outlets also abound in the neighborhood; for a good resource on outlet shopping pick up a copy of *Bargain Hunting in the Bay Area* by Sally Socolich.

Historic **Jackson Square**, on the edge of the Financial District, specializes in pricey antiques displayed in appropriately antique surroundings.

With over 100 specialty shops, restaurants, and guided tours, it's no wonder Pier 39 keeps packing them in.

Chinatown is a seething bazaar where the choice of exotica is overwhelming – from an abacus to X-rated fortune cookies.

Embarcadero Center – like Chinatown, another city-within-the-city – is an urban redevelopment project similar in scale to the Rockefeller Plaza in New York, with more than 150 shops among the offices, restaurants, cafés, sculptures, and bright flower-filled pots.

North Beach, birthplace of the beatniks, specializes in offbeat shops and genuinely interesting bookshops, including the famous City Lights. Also eccentric is **Haight Street**, the main thoroughfare of the one-time flower-power Haight-Ashbury district, with nostalgia rampant in the shops.

Union Street, an area of Victorian-era houses, has since been upgraded into a smart shopping zone of stylish boutiques, accessories for home and body, and lots of restaurants. Same for **Fillmore Street**, which contains some only-in-San-Francisco gems.

Fisherman's Wharf is geared strictly toward tourists with sweatshirt emporiums and dubious art that lines Jefferson Street and spills into **Pier 39**. A better choice is **Ghirardelli Square**, a 19th-century factory complex overlooking the bay, which has been converted into a tasteful array of shops, galleries, and restaurants. **The Cannery** also has three floors of shops, cafés, and attractions in an 1890s former peach cannery across the street.

What to Buy

San Francisco is a great place to shop for art, high-quality crafts, clothing, items for the home, and wine. Be sure to browse offbeat galleries and gift shops where many local

With the second largest Chinese community outside Asia, Chinatown lets you visit Asia without leaving the country.

artists provide everything from funky jewelry and handbags fashioned from antique kimonos to hand-painted furniture.

Books: Writing, reading, and publishing books are venerable traditions in San Francisco.

Clothing: Sportswear and casual styles are the best bet. Blue jeans fans should check out the Levi's store on Union Square where customers can personally soak themselves and their new jeans in a "shrink-to-fit" tank.

Food and drink: Sourdough bread is wrapped "to go" at the airport – handy if you've a long wait. Also, San Francisco chocolates, candies, and salami make good portable souvenirs. Or why not take home a bottle of fine California wine?

Gadgets: There is always be something new and fascinating for the kitchen, car, or office to be found in San Francisco. If it's electrical, make sure the equipment can be adapted to the voltage back at home.

Sporting goods: It's worth pricing the golf and tennis equipment, and don't forget to take home a baseball cap.

Toys: Both big and little shops sell the latest in toys, games, and educational gifts.

SPORTS

Never too hot, never too cool, the climate encourages sporting people of many disciplines to excel year round. Only the swimming can be problematic. The beaches may be beautiful, but the tides are treacherous, the water cold, and the fog can cast a pall.

Golf: There are six public courses, including the 18-hole Presidio green opened to the public in 1995 (Tel: 415-561-4653). For golf as well as inspiring views, try out the Lincoln Park (Tel: 415-750-GOLF) or Harding Park (Tel: 415-664-4690) courses. If you've come to California for the golfing experience of your life, Pebble Beach is less than 3 hours by car south of San Francisco.

Tennis: There are over 100 well-maintained tennis courts in parks around San Francisco that are city-run and free – first come, first served. (The courts at Dolores Park on Dolores and 18th Street are lighted at night.) A fee is charged for the 21 courts in Golden Gate Park. At the top end of the market, the San Francisco Tennis Club at 645 Fifth Street (Tel: 415-777-9000) has indoor and outdoor courts as well as exercise facilities.

Rainy Day Pastimes

San Francisco weather is usually mild, but in case wind, rain, or fog make outdoor activities too chilly, there are fine indoor alternatives. The five-story Sony Metreon at Yerba Buena Gardens is filled with activities, including 15 movie theaters, numerous restaurants, a virtual games room and shopping opportunities. Museums are also perfect havens during wet weather, especially the Museum of Modern Art on Third Street or the California Academy of Science in Golden Gate Park. A thorough look through the exhibits can be followed by a bite to eat and a stroll through the gift shop. Around Union Square, the Rotunda restaurant at Neiman Marcus, and the Sheraton Palace and Westin St Francis hotels all serve afternoon tea in lovely surroundings.

For a respite from exploring the city, take to the beach,
where you can ride the tide or stroll the coast.

Cycling: Yet another San Francisco advantage, with all the scenic surroundings available. There are two bike routes: one through Golden Gate Park to the Great Highway, the other from the southern part of the city to the Golden Gate Bridge. Rental shops are to be found alongside the park.

Jogging: Golden Gate Park is a favorite, but you might like to experience the 5-mile path around Lake Merced, or the bay views from the Marina Green, or parallel the Pacific on Ocean Beach. Serious runners can compete in the San Francisco Marathon, or the costume-optional Bay to Breakers Run.

Hiking: There are many beautiful hiking trails on Mt. Tam across the bay in Marin, but you don't have to leave the city to break in your boots. For views and a challenging walk, take the **Coastal Trail** from Fort Point (underneath the Golden Gate Bridge) to the Cliff House; but don't climb on the cliffs themselves, as they aren't stable. Eight miles from the shore, **Angel Island** sports a dozen miles of trails; ride the Blue and Gold Ferry and take a picnic lunch.

Boating: For bay boating, with or without a licensed captain, see the charter firms along the Embarcadero or in Sausalito. The Blue and Gold fleet (Tel: 415-773-1188) offers one-hour bay cruises that under the Golden Gate Bridge and around Alcatraz and Angel islands. Other firms combine dining with sailing, including The Ruby (Tel: 415-861-2165) and Hornblower Dining Yachts (Tel: 415-788-8866).

Fishing: Several deep-sea fishing companies operate out of Fisherman's Wharf. Boats leave early in the morning in search of salmon, bass, or whatever is running. If seasickness is a problem, consider casting a line from Municipal Pier in Aquatic Park.

If you need an escape from the throngs of tourists on the pier, Aquatic Park has a fine beach for all the family.

Spectator Sports

Baseball: One of the great American pastimes unfolds, slowly, at the spiffy new Pacific Bell Park, when the San Francisco Giants are in town. Seating is limited to 40,000, so tickets may be difficult to come by. Across the bridge, the A's play at the Oakland Coliseum.

Basketball: Big-time basketball takes over after the baseball season ends. The Golden State Warriors of the National Basketball Association's Pacific Division entertain in Oakland Coliseum.

Football: Named after the gold rush invaders, the powerful San Francisco '49ers of the National Football League are based at 3Com Park at Candlestick Point. The season runs from August to December. Tickets are nearly impossible to get. The Oakland Raiders are also worth watching, or catch a college game – Stanford University is often one of the nation's top teams.

Horse racing: The nearest thoroughbred racing is held at Golden Gate Fields (Tel: 510-559-7300) in Albany, north of Berkeley off Interstate 80. Twenty minutes south on Highway 101 is Bay Meadows in San Mateo (Tel: 650-574-7223). The horse-racing season takes place all year, alternating between these two fields.

CHILDREN'S SAN FRANCISCO

Frank Sinatra aptly described San Francisco as a "grown-up, swinging town," but it's equally swinging for kids. If anyone needs an impromptu push, few parks are bereft of play structures, and what child, small or large, would deny the true excitement of a ride on the cable cars?

No parent can resist the chance to inculcate his offspring

Climb on board the historic ships of Hyde Street Pier for a glimpse into maritime history.

with a little culture, and there are a number of exciting museums that will do the trick without raising resistance from the kids. For example, the made-for-children **Exploratorium** (Tel: 415-561-0360) is one of the finest science museums in the world and full of hands-on exhibits to suit all ages.

Also very popular is the **California Academy of Sciences** in Golden Gate Park (Tel: 415-750-7145), which hosts traveling exhibits along with enduring animal dioramas and has a nifty aquarium where kids can investigate starfish and sea urchins. The planetarium shows at Morrison Planetarium inside the academy (Tel: 415-750-7141) are also entertaining. Other park attractions include a huge playground and charming carousel. South of Market, **Zeum** (Tel: 415-777-2800) at Yerba Buena Gardens is a fascinating technology center geared toward older kids and teens with an interest in computers, art, and video. Nearby on Fourth Street is the **Cartoon Art Museum** (Tel: 415-227-8666) with exhibits on underground and mainstream comics.

Ice skating and **bowling** are other youthful favorites at Yerba Buena Gardens, and neither require advance reservations. **The Metreon** itself is a kid magnet with its Airtight Garage, interactive video games, movies, and shops. Farther afield, the 65-acre **San Francisco Zoo** (Tel: 415-753-7080) is home to over 1,000 animals and has a zoo train and a large playground. A visit to Ocean Beach can be combined with a stop at the charming **Musée Mécanique** below the Cliff House (Tel: 415-386-1170). This small museum is loaded with fantastically restored mechanical toys and games that were the forerunners to pinball and video machines. Bring along a roll of quarters.

Down near **Fisherman's Wharf** and **Aquatic Park** are seaworthy places to spend time with the kids, including inside the WWII submarine *U.S.S. Pampanito* (Tel: 415-775-1943) and the **Hyde Street Pier** (Tel: 415-561-7100), home to a historic ships open for tours.

If the weather turns ugly during your stay in the city, you could turn to **The Cannery** where your children can create a new stuffed pal at the **Basic Brown Bear Factory** (Tel: 415-931-6670) or paint ceramics at **Handmade Ceramic Studio** (Tel: 415-440-2898).

On the Beaches

If you don't mind brisk temperatures, go ahead and dip your toes in the Pacific Ocean. Here are some sandy beaches, reading from north to south:

Baker Beach, part of the Presidio, is highly unsafe for swimming but popular with joggers, picnickers, and sunbathers (nude ones on the northern portion).

China Beach, also known as Phelan Beach, is a protected cove where swimming is permitted; lifeguards are on duty during the warmer months.

Ocean Beach runs on and on alongside the Great Highway south from the Cliff House. Swimming can be quite dangerous, but the sand and sunsets are superb.

Festivals

Parades, street fairs, and celebrations of the most exotic types occur with great frequency in San Francisco. Some of the highlights to note are:

February–March: Chinese New Year: fireworks, dragon dances, and a parade through Chinatown. St. Patrick's Day parade, downtown. The Martin Luther King Birthday Celebration.

April: Cherry Blossom Festival, Japantown. S.F. International Film Festival, various locations around town.

May: Cinco de Mayo (5 May) Mexican fiesta and parade, Mission District. Carnival (Memorial Day weekend): a wild parade and festival featuring samba dancers, food, crafts, music, Mission District.

June: Gay Freedom Day parade to the Civic Center. Union Street Fair, arts and crafts on Union between Fillmore and Gough Streets. North Beach Festival, the oldest urban street fair, North Beach.

July: Fourth of July fireworks along the waterfront. San Francisco Flower Show in Golden Gate Park. Jazz and All That Art on Fillmore, Fillmore Street between Post and Jackson streets.

August: A La Carte, A La Park: food festival with great music in Golden Gate Park.

September: Blues Festival at Fort Mason, and the renowned Shakespeare festival in Golden Gate Park. Autumn Moon Festival in Chinatown. Festival de las Americas, Mission District.

October: Columbus Day parade, Italian-American Festival in North Beach. Castro Street Fair. Exotic-Erotic Ball on Halloween. Jazz Festival.

November: Day of the Dead Festival, Mission District. Bay Area Book Festival, Fort Mason.

EATING OUT

You don't have to be a connoisseur of unusual comestibles, exotic sauces, or esoteric ethnic flavors to appreciate San Francisco's restaurant world. People who really care about food start with the basics: Is the bread worth eating, the fish freshly landed, the salad crisp? In San Francisco the answer is yes, yes, and yes. Thus gourmets can turn to more sophisticated realms, which are extraordinarily rewarding here – including the wines.

The success of the San Francisco food scene can be summed up in just one word: abundance. Thousands of restaurants, representing almost every cuisine under the sun, exploit a cornucopia of natural ingredients fresh from the sea and California's rich farming zones. Local gourmets have developed great expectations, which inspires ever greater achievements by the chefs, some of whom are nationally renowned personalities.

Here, as in most big cities, restaurants come and go. Those that survive cater to all tastes and pocketbooks and in all styles. San Francisco is a food-conscious metropolis, and ethnic restaurants in particular offer value so good that you could spend your time here without ever stepping foot into a fast-food joint.

If you're keen to sample typical American fare, you'll also find every regional delight from Boston clam chowder to Cajun blackened fish, from a Chicago T-bone steak to New York deli sandwiches. But San Francisco shimmers when it comes to California cuisine. Inspiring many Northern California restaurant kitchens is the influence of Alice Waters of Chez Panisse fame *(see page 141)*. Cooking and eating as a lifestyle choice developed out of this Berkeley institution and Waters decisively helped jump-start the move

With pleasant weather year-round, people try to spend as much time outside as possible – a quick bite at a cable car café.

to organic farming. Now, small local producers of everything from heirloom tomatoes and baby lettuces to olive oil and free-range chickens deliver to the back doors of small and large establishments, whose menus vary depending on what's in season.

As for foreign food, San Francisco may well have no rival for sheer variety, due chiefly to its Pacific outlook. Every American city has Chinese restaurants, but where else could you choose among Cantonese, Mandarin, Shanghainese, Taiwanese, Hakka, and at least half-a-dozen other schools of Chinese cooking? Hong Kong perhaps – but there you'd have trouble tracking down real Mexican, Russian, Basque, and Ethiopian cuisine, offered here as well.

Customs and Coffee

Small-town Americans have dinner as early as 5pm, even when they come to San Francisco, but it's more fashionable to dine after 7pm, and most restaurants stay open to 10pm or later. Breakfast is served from about 7 to about 10am, though in many establishments breakfast specialties such as pancakes and scrambled eggs are served all day long. Lunch is usually served between noon and 2pm.

Coffee appears to be the local drink of choice based on the fact that coffee bars take up more real estate than even Gap clothing stores (which you'll also find on nearly every street corner). Once you order your tall lowfat, no-foam latte with a sprinkle of cocoa, you're on your own. But in restaurants, your waiter will appear with great frequency to inquire if you'd like a refill of java. Thus you may dilute your meal with several cups for the price of one, if caffeine is your thing.

Tipping is straightforward. Before all the taxes have been added to the bill ("the check"), calculate 15–20 percent of the total and allocate it to the waiter or waitress, up to 25 percent in the case of extraordinary service. In many informal eateries you pay the cashier on the way out, leaving a tip on the table or in a tip jar located on the counter.

Specialties

The big drawing card in San Francisco is the **seafood**, so wholesome that it doesn't take a famous chef to do it justice. **Dungeness Crab** is the local specialty. It is available from mid-November to May and is served in many forms – Newburg, steamed fresh, au gratin, or, less elegantly, as morsels assembled as takeaway snacks in plastic cups. Other shellfish that grace the menu are shrimp, oysters, scallops, and mussels.

One part-seafood dish even comes with its own legend. The wryly named **Hangtown Fry** – scrambled eggs, ham, and oysters – is said to have been devised in gold rush days by a gallows-bound prisoner in Placerville. In his request for a last meal, the wily criminal chose ingredients that would take some time to assemble.

Seafood also figures in many of the ethnic restaurants. **Cioppino**, an Italian-descended seafood stew, is claimed as a San Francisco original. Thai restaurants serve spicy crab salad, Chinese chefs immerse lobster in black bean sauce, and fresh scallops and prawns appear in Japanese *sushi*.

Fresh fish from the broad Pacific is another of San Francisco's advantages. Swordfish, salmon, tuna, and seabass are meaty enough to satisfy even the most deter-

Drawing on the city's rich multi-cultural heritage, the local cuisine will satisfy the most adventurous palates.

mined carnivore. The giant fish are sliced into steaks, while smaller ones are usually filleted. In the United States, fish are normally served minus heads and tails.

Meat eaters can start with steaks in their all-American diversity – Porterhouse, *filet mignon*, T-bone. Roast beef, veal, lamb, and pork round out the menu. In the meantime, don't underestimate the great American hamburger.

For **vegetarians** California offers a better choice than almost anywhere else. Not only are the ingredients impeccable, but there's an understanding of nutritional requirements. There are a handful of vegetarian eateries in town, and a few achieve gourmet level; almost all local restaurants have creative vegetarian dishes on the menu.

Desserts include some sensational fresh fruits. Pies and cakes are as rich as you can stand them, and the ice-cream, in a truly bewildering array of flavors, is an inspiration. Only a few upscale restaurants have cheeses on the dessert menu, although the list is growing.

California Wine

California's wine-makers have added the advantages of science and technology to an already blessed climate, assuring consistently superior results. Scientists at the University of California at Davis have bred new hybrid grapes with names like Ruby Cabernet and Centurion, designed to upgrade hitherto boring table wines. Visiting wine aficionados will enjoy tracking down world-class vintages. To the ordinary diner, the California revolution simply means that even the least pompous house wine is eminently drinkable. Wine can be ordered by the glass or bottle.

Every sort of wine produced in Europe, from **Sherry** and **Champagne**-style sparkling wine to **Port** and **brandy**, has its equivalent in California – plus Japanese *sake,* distilled from local rice and served in sushi bars and Japanese restaurants.

Labels identify the winery, the region, the variety of grape, the vintage year if appropriate, and alcoholic content. Classic European grapes like Cabernet Sauvignon and Pinot Noir are represented, along with less-familiar hybrids like Gamay Beaujolais. California's vineyards stretch all the way from San Diego county, where the Spanish friars planted the first grapes in 1769, to Mendocino in the cool north.

You don't have to be an expert in varietals and vintages to enjoy forays in the Sonoma and Napa valleys, the wine zones most easily accessible from San Francisco *(see pages 69–72).* Take advantage of the tastings and tours offered by many of the popular wineries.

Other Drinks

In cosmopolitan San Francisco people drink Scotch whisky or Polish vodka, Irish coffee or Mexican tequila, as well as a

---

By Bread Alone

You'd have to go to Paris to find a bread remotely as tasty as San Francisco's **sourdough**. Many a tourist carry home souvenir loaves.

What makes sourdough bread so good is the secret ingredient descended from a micro-organism brought from Europe in time for the gold rush. Prospectors carried small quantities of this "starter" of fermented dough to cause the bread they baked in the wilds to rise. A bit of this same bacillus is recycled every day in the complex process used by the bakeries of San Francisco. Sourer or sweeter, darker or lighter, according to your choice, the crusty end-product can be a meal in itself.

Since its days as a chocolate factory, Ghirardelli Square has managed to transform itself into an all-out shopping hotspot.

staggering range of **cocktails.** One of the best perhaps is a **margarita** – iced tequila with Cointreau or Triple Sec, lime juice, and a coating of salt around the rim of the glass.

Beer, domestic or imported, is normally served very cold in glasses or mugs. There are "micro breweries" all over town, where you can admire to gleaming tanks and taste various styles of beer and ale produced on the premises. San Francisco's contribution to the science of beer-making is "steam beer," an historic method of brewing using air cooling rather than ice.

Health faddists, who seem to abound in California, may prefer to sip brand-name mineral waters, perhaps with a sliver of low-calorie lime, or fresh **fruit juices** with a dollop of protein powder blended at specialty juice bars that grace most neighborhoods.

HANDY TRAVEL TIPS

An A–Z Summary of Practical Information

A

ACCOMMODATIONS (see also CAMPING, YOUTH HOSTELS, and the list of Recommended Hotels starting on page 125)

Some of the world's finest and most famous hotels contribute to San Francisco's reputation for hospitality. These exclusive hotels compete on the basis of their international reputations and such "little extras" as discreet concierges, complimentary limousine service, fresh flowers, and twice-daily maid service. One of them (the Westin St. Francis) even runs a "money laundering" operation to be sure all the coins handed to guests are impeccably clean and shiny. Of course, most of the 30,000 hotel rooms on the city's books are more modest, but charm and comfort persist far down the line from the luxury class.

Hotel chains such as the Marriott, Hyatt, and Hilton are well represented, as are more intimate "boutique" hotels and bed-and-breakfast establishments. It's always wise to have advance reservations. Most hotels have toll-free telephone numbers, but keep in mind that they can only be dialed from within the United States.

All hotel rates in San Francisco are subject to a 14 percent room tax. Parking downtown can add another $10 to $25 per day, and telephone surcharges will also inflate the bill.

For a free Lodging Guide published annually by the San Francisco Convention & Visitors Bureau contact the bureau, Tel: (415) 391-9974 (toll-free in US) or write to them at 900 Market Street, San Francisco, CA 94103-2804.

AIRPORTS

San Francisco International Airport has the auspicious title of the seventh-busiest airport in the world, handling about 1,300 flights per day. The airport is on the freeway 14 miles (23 km) south of the city – half an hour by taxi but a bit longer during the rush hour. A major expansion project, due for completion around 2006, aims to ease the crowding in the efficient but overstretched terminal and will add a BART station. Information booths, with multilingual staff, are located near baggage claim areas in each terminal. No airport or departure taxes are collected from travelers.

Taxis are always available outside the doors of the arrival area. The fare to downtown is around $30 plus tip. Shuttle vans are available at center islands outside the upper-level departure terminals. They provide door-to-door service for $13–15 (before tip) per person; advance reservations are not necessary. If you are renting a car, a courtesy bus will deposit you at the new, rather inefficient rental car building where all the rental counters and cars are located.

An alternative to SFO Airport is the less hectic Oakland International Airport across the Bay. A shuttle bus links the airport to the BART rapid transit line *(see page 119)* to downtown San Francisco. Otherwise, taxis and shuttle buses are available outside the airline terminals.

B

BICYCLE RENTAL
There are miles of agreeable cycling routes in Golden Gate Park, and on Sundays John F. Kennedy Drive is closed to automobile traffic so you can cycle nearly to the beach free of exhaust fumes. Bikes may be hired on Stanyan Street near the park's eastern boundary for around $5 per hour. Cycling across the Golden Gate Bridge is also enjoyable (if windy), and at least one rental company (Bay Bicycle Tours in the Cannery; Tel: 415-923-6434) offers a bike tour to Sausalito with a return trip by ferry. Cycling is a popular way of exploring the wine country north of San Francisco, with rentals and tours available in Sonoma, St. Helena, and Calistoga.

BUDGETING for YOUR TRIP
San Francisco isn't an inexpensive destination. The average daily expenditure per visitor is over $130 according to the Convention &

Visitors Bureau, with the bulk of expenses divided between lodging and food. While many hotels offer weekend and off-season rates, there isn't a true low season in the city.

Accommodations. Plan to pay from $100 for a modest motel room outside Union Square to $185 on up for a small but smartly decorated room at the city's finer boutique hotels. Then add 14 percent room tax and another $20 or so, per day, if you plan to park a car downtown. Hotels closer to the Tenderloin tend to be less expensive, but if you want to save on accommodations, consider instead places in outlying neighborhoods, such as the Sunset, that are close to public transportation. On the web, <www.bay area.citysearch.com> is a good resource for listings.

Meals. You can eat well without blowing your entire budget although it will be tempting to splurge for at least one superb dinner while you're here. Ethnic restaurants in the Mission District, Chinatown, Japantown, and the Richmond District are generally quite inexpensive and offer a wonderful opportunity to sample cuisines from around the world. You can easily spend under $15 per person for a great Chinese, Mexican, Salvadoran, Vietnamese, Thai, or Japanese meal (among others) by exploring these neighborhoods.

Transportation. Driving a car in the city is an expensive and aggravating proposition. If possible, use public transportation and taxis while inside the city limits. Buses and Muni cost $1 and you'll receive a transfer good for a second trip within 2 hours. Cab fare runs $2 for the first mile then $1.80 per mile. Parking fees are hefty downtown and at Fisherman's Wharf where the major lot charges $5 per hour.

Attractions. Some of the best attractions in town are free, including the Golden Gate Bridge, Chinatown, and Strybing Arboretum in Golden Gate Park. Museum admissions begin at $7 for adults (nearly half for kids), and a daytime tour to Alcatraz will set a couple back almost $25.

C

CAMPING

There are campsites in state parks outside San Francisco in Marin County and Half Moon Bay, but camping is not allowed in the city. For information, write to California Department of Parks and Recreation, Attention Publications Office, PO Box 942896, Sacramento, CA 94296. National Parks Service information is available from Building 201, Fort Mason, San Francisco, CA 94123. For addresses and telephone numbers of commercial campgrounds for recreational vehicles see the *Yellow Pages* under "Campgrounds & Recreational Vehicle Parks."

CAR RENTAL/HIRE

Driving and parking in the city can be an unpleasant experience at best and if you can avoid renting a car, do so. For trips outside the city, rent on an as-needed basis from one of the many firms located around Union Square. Car rental companies compete for business, so it's worth shopping around if you have the time and patience. At the airport and downtown, every national firm is represented (Avis, Budget, Hertz, National) as well as smaller local companies such as Enterprise. Prices vary widely under the laws of supply and demand, according to the season, and even within a single firm on the same day. Look into special weekly and weekend rates and Internet specials, but budget about $40 per day, not including parking fees.

Automatic transmission and air-conditioning are standard. Note that rates which sound reasonable can end up much higher when insurance is added. Check your auto insurance policy to see if you are fully covered for rentals before accepting the "collision damage waiver" option. This insurance will add $10 per day or more to the cost. Also, you'll probably save if you hire a car with unlimited mileage.

Renters need a valid driver's license plus an International Driving Permit if you reside outside the US or Canada. Most agencies set a minimum age for car rental at 25, some at 21 and a credit card is required.

CLIMATE

The biggest surprise for visitors is that summer can be very chilly. Those people shivering in shorts are uninformed tourists. If they had driven an hour inland they might be sweltering in tropical sunshine, but the famous fog transmits cold ocean temperatures into the city. Oddly, the warmest season is autumn. Of course, it doesn't take much to constitute a heat wave in San Francisco. Winters are cold, often rainy, and sometimes windy.

To help you with long-range predictions, here are the average daily maximum and minimum temperatures by month for San Francisco.

	J	F	M	A	M	J	J	A	S	O	N	D
maximum												
°F	55	59	61	62	63	66	65	65	69	68	63	57
°C	13	15	16	17	17	19	18	18	21	20	17	14
minimum												
°F	45	47	48	49	51	52	53	53	55	54	51	47
°C	7	8	9	9	11	11	12	12	13	12	11	8

CLOTHING

A sweater or jacket is likely to be welcome for at least part of every day in San Francisco, even during what the rest of the northern hemisphere knows as summer. Generally, mid-weight clothing is the best bet year-round, though an all-weather coat will come in handy in winter. Comfortable walking shoes go a long way toward taming the hills. Like the rest of California, San Franciscans have succumbed to an informal dress code. The best restaurants require a coat for gentlemen, but casual clothes are acceptable nearly everywhere you go.

San Francisco

COMPLAINTS

If you have a serious complaint about business practices, first talk to the manager of the establishment. Should this fail to resolve the problem, try the Better Business Bureau, 114 Sansome Street, Suite 1103; Tel: (415) 243-9999.

CRIME & SAFETY

With a relatively low crime rate for a large city, San Francisco poses no special dangers. However, the lack of gun control in the US means that in general, criminals are more dangerous. Take cabs late at night, don't walk unescorted in the wee hours, and avoid the mysteries of dark streets or run-down areas. Leave valuables in your hotel safe, and beware of pickpockets in crowded places and on Muni. If you have a car, don't leave anything inside in plain sight and always lock the doors. The all-purpose emergency telephone number is **911.** For less urgent police business, Tel: (415) 553-0123.

CUSTOMS & ENTRY REQUIREMENTS

For a stay of less than 90 days, British visitors with a valid ten-year passport and a return ticket on a major airline do not generally need a US visa. Nationals of most other European countries are given the same priority. Canadian visitors merely have to show proof of nationality. Citizens of Australia, Portugal, and South Africa need a visa, but rules do change, so check with your local US embassy or consulate, or with your travel agent.

If you do need a visa, application forms are available through travel agents, airlines, or US consulates. Allow at least a month for postal applications. Forms must be accompanied by a passport valid for at least six months longer than the intended visit, a passport-size photo, evidence of possession of sufficient funds, and proof of intent to leave the US after the visit. A health certificate is not normally required.

Red and green channels are in use at America's international airports and all formalities are simpler and quicker than in the past. If you fly in, you should be given the customs and immigration forms to complete well before landing.

Duty-free allowance. The following chart shows certain duty-free items a non-resident may take into the US (if you are over 21) and, when returning home, into your own country.

Into:	Cigarettes		Cigars		Tobacco	Spirits		Wine
US	200	or	50	or	1,350g	1 l	or	1 l
Australia	200	or	250	or	250g	1 l	or	1 l
Canada	200	and	50	and	900g	1.14 l	or	1.14 l
Ireland	200	or	50	or	150g	1 l	and	2 l
New Zealand	200	or	50	or	250g	1.1 l	and	4.5 l
South Africa	400	and	50	and	250g	1 l	and	2 l
UK	200	or	50	or	250g	1 l	and	2 l

A non-resident may take into the US gifts, free of duty and taxes, to a value of $100. The import of plants, seeds, vegetables, fruits, or other fresh food is prohibited; foods of all kinds are subject to inspection. If you're carrying money and checks totaling more than $10,000 in or out of the country, they must be reported.

DRIVING

The United States is the land of the car, but when it comes to San Francisco the best advice is "don't" – except for out-of-town trips. The hills and parking problems exacerbate the normal hazards of city driving.

The regulations are straightforward. Drive on the right, pass on the left. Unless there's a sign to the contrary, you can turn right on a red signal, providing that you stop and check that no pedestrians or traffic deter this maneuver. Drivers and all passengers must wear seatbelts; children under 4 years require child restraints. Cable cars always have the right of way, as do pedestrians at the designated crosswalks. School buses (painted yellow) are given special priority by law; it is a serious offense to pass a school bus *in either direction* on a two-lane road when it is taking on or discharging passengers.

Highways. California has no toll roads, though you have to pay to cross the Golden Gate Bridge or the San Francisco-Oakland Bay Bridge. (Fares are collected only as you arrive in San Francisco.) The freeway system is complicated enough to deserve advanced planning; if you miss an exit you can lose a lot of time trying to double back.

Speed limits. On Interstate highways the limit is normally 65 mph (105 km/h). On all other highways the limit is 55 mph (90 km/h).

Parking. "Curbing" the wheels of a parked car is the law in San Francisco, so that if a car rolls downhill the curb will brake it. Parking downhill, turn your wheels toward the curb; parking uphill, away from the curb. Engage the handbrake and put the car in gear. Parking meters govern the time you can stay in some areas and many only accept quarters. Elsewhere in the city a color code indicates the restrictions. A red curb means no parking at all, green represents a 10-minute parking limit, yellow is a loading zone, and a white curb is a no-parking zone permitting passenger loading only. The tow-trucks mean business, especially if you block a fire hydrant or a bus stop. Read the posted signs on all streets for street cleaning days and other parking restrictions, including no parking rules on downtown streets between 3 and 6pm.

Fuel. Most gas (petrol) stations are self-service and are equipped to accept credit cards for payment at the pump. "Full-serve" is more expensive, but it may include a window cleaning. Gas stations are open every day from early in the morning until 10pm or later.

Breakdowns and services. The American Automobile Association (AAA) offers assistance to members of affiliated organizations abroad. It also provides travel information for the US and can arrange automobile insurance by the month for owner-drivers. In San Francisco the AAA-affiliated automobile club is the California State Automobile Association, 150 Van Ness Avenue; Tel: (415) 565-2012. In case of breakdown, dial (800) AAA-Help (toll-free) for information on how to obtain emergency assistance.

Fluid measures

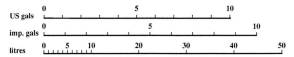

Distance

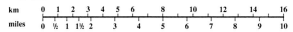

E

EARTHQUAKES

Basically, the Bay Area is in the line of fire. If you feel a tremor while you're indoors, stay there, preferably in a door frame. Outdoors, avoid trees, power lines, and the walls of buildings. In a car, sit it out by the side of the road, but away from power lines and bridges. If you want to be prepared for the worst, study the San Francisco telephone directory, which contains four pages of earthquake instructions. If you'd like to find out what a tremor feels like, stop by the California Academy of Sciences and check out the earthquake exhibit.

ELECTRICITY

Throughout the United States the standard is 110 volts, 60 cycle AC. Plugs have two flat prongs. Overseas visitors without dual-voltage travel appliances will need a transformer and adapter plug for appliances such as an electric razor or a hair dryer.

San Francisco

EMBASSIES & CONSULATES
All embassies in the US are in Washington, DC, but some countries also maintain consulates in San Francisco. To find the address of a consulate, look in the alphabetical listings of the telephone directory under "Consulates" or in the *Yellow Pages* under "Consulates and Other Foreign Government Representatives."

Australia: 1 Bush Street, Suite 1103; Tel: (415) 536-1970.

Canada: 550 South Hope Street, Los Angeles; Tel: (213) 346-2700.

Ireland: 100 Pine Street, Suite 3830; Tel: (415) 392-4214.

New Zealand: 1 Maritime Plaza; Tel: (415) 399-1255.

South Africa: 6300 Wilshire Blvd, Suite 600, Los Angeles 90048; Tel: (323) 651-0902.

United Kingdom: 1 Sansome Street, Suite 850; Tel: (415) 617-1300.

EMERGENCIES (see also HEALTH, MEDICAL CARE, & POLICE)
Call the all-purpose emergency number, 911, from any telephone; no coins are required. The operator will note the information and relay it to the police, ambulance, or the fire department, accordingly.

G

GAY & LESBIAN TRAVELERS
San Francisco is, arguably, the "gayest" city in the US. Most of the scene is concentrated in the Castro neighborhood, but you will find gay places all over town. The *Bay Area Reporter* has the most comprehensive listings and is available free. Most of the lesbian community is centered around Valencia Street and Noe Valley.

GETTING THERE
By Air. Dozens of international flights serve San Francisco daily. The major carriers offer non-stop flights from Europe to San Francisco, or connections via New York, Chicago, or Los Angeles. There are non-stop or one-stop flights from the principal Pacific airports. Beyond the

standard first class, business/club, and economy fares, the principal cost-cutting possibilities are variations of APEX (book 21 days before departure for stays of 7 days to 6 months). Off-season reduced fares and package deals are also available. Certain US airlines offer bargains for foreign travelers who visit several American destinations.

From North America, direct flights connect American and Canadian cities to San Francisco. Special fares are available on these highly competitive routes and prices frequently change. Fly-drive vacations, including flight, hotel, and rental car, are offered by many airlines.

By Rail. Amtrak, the passenger railway company, goes only as far as Oakland, where special shuttle buses take passengers to the Ferry Building at Market and Embarcadero streets in San Francisco. The *California Zephyr* links Oakland with Chicago and Denver. The *Coast Starlight* stops in Oakland on the way from Portland and Seattle to Los Angeles and San Diego. Amtrak offers special package tours. Travelers who are permanent residents of countries outside the United States and Canada are eligible to buy USA Rail Passes covering 45 days of unlimited travel on Amtrak. If your travel agent lacks the information, write to Amtrak International Sales, 60 Massachusetts Avenue, NE, Washington, DC 20002. In the US, telephone (800) USA-RAIL (toll-free); <www.amtrak.com>.

By Bus. Long-distance Greyhound-Trailways buses use the Transbay Terminal. For more information about bus services across the continent, telephone Greyhound-Trailways toll-free at (800) 231-2222; <www.greyhound.com>.

By Car. The excellent Interstate freeway system criss-crosses all of the United States. Odd numbers designate freeways running north to south, while even-numbered interstates run east to west. Interstate 101, for instance, serves the length of California, entering San Francisco via the Golden Gate Bridge and leaving near the airport.

GUIDES & TOURS

San Francisco tour companies offer bus, boat, bike, and foot excursions aimed at the broadest or narrowest interest, from a one-hour glimpse of the city's highlights aboard a simulated cable car to a walking (and eating and shopping) tour of Chinatown or the Castro. Leaflets listing the possibilities proliferate in hotel lobbies and the Visitor Information Center at Powell and Market streets. Some tour companies are geared to providing guides who speak foreign languages, but advance notice may be required. Bargain hunters and anyone interested in the history of San Francisco should contact City Guides (Tel: 415-557-4266; <www.sfcityguides.org>) for information on their 35 free weekly walking tours.

H

HEALTH & MEDICAL CARE

Everywhere in the United States health care is extremely expensive, especially hospitalization, which can quickly become an economic disaster. It is essential, before you leave home, to sign up for medical insurance covering your stay. This can be arranged through an insurance company or agent or through your travel agent as part of a travel insurance package. Foreign visitors in need may wish to ask their consulate for a list of doctors.

Tap water is perfectly safe to drink everywhere in the Bay Area.

Drugstores (pharmacies). Many drugstores of the Walgreen chain stay open 24 hours a day; in others, pharmacists are available until midnight. Check with your hoTel: You may find that some medicines obtainable over the counter in your home country are available only by prescription in the US, and vice versa.

HOLIDAYS

Banks, post offices, government buildings, and some businesses are closed on the following major holidays:

1 January	New Years Day
Third Monday in January	Martin Luther King Day
Third Monday in February	Presidents' Day
Last Monday in May	Memorial Day
4 July	Independence Day
First Monday in September	Labor Day
Second Monday in October	Columbus Day
11 November	Veterans' Day
Last Thursday in November	Thanksgiving
25 December	Christmas Day

I

INTERNET CAFÉS

You can check your email while on the road at The CoffeeNet, 744 Harrison Street, Tel: 415-567-5888 (between 3rd and 4th streets), open for java and internet access Mon–Fri 8am–7pm, Sat 10am–5pm; and Cafe.com, 970 Market Street (near Mason Street, Tel: 415-922-5322), open Mon–Fri, 6am–midnight, Sun 7am–10pm.

L

LANGUAGE

American English is spoken here. You will also here Chinese, Japanese, Spanish, Russian, and many other languages, as San Francisco is a cosmopolitan city.

LAUNDRY & DRY CLEANING

Express laundry and dry-cleaning services are available at most hotels, though this is expensive. If money is a factor, you can seek out a neighborhood laundry or cleaning establishment; same-day or even one-hour service may be offered. Laundromats (launderettes), self-service establishments with coin-operated washing machines and dryers, are a cheaper alternative. One bold step beyond the laundromat is an establishment called Brain Wash at 1122 Folsom Street, which adds food, drink, and music to the wash-and-dry formula; open until 11pm.

LIQUOR LAWS

Liquor is sold in supermarkets and even some drugstores, but not between 2am and 6am. The same schedule restrictions affect restaurants and bars; some can serve only beer and wine. You may be asked to prove you are 21, the legal age for drinking in California.

M

MAPS

Various cartographic companies publish detailed maps of San Francisco which are sold at bookstores, news kiosks, and gas stations. A comprehensive map of the city's streets and public transport system is sold by Muni, the San Francisco Municipal Railway. Free tourist magazines usually include maps of the most popular areas.

MEDIA

The major daily newspaper in town is the *San Francisco Chronicle*. Delivered in the morning, it is available from sidewalk kiosks and often at your hotel's front desk. Almost every hotel room has radio and television with a vast choice of programs. Broadcasting is a round-the-clock business, and in San Francisco that includes a wide range of foreign languages. The nationwide commercial networks are found on channels 2, 4, 5, and 7, and channel 9 is the local affiliate of Public Broadcasting Service (PBS), with higher quality output as a rule, and commercial-free. Most hotels have cable TV.

On the radio, dial 810AM for news, weather and traffic reports.

MONEY

Currency. The dollar ($) is divided into 100 cents (¢).

Banknotes: $1, $5, $10, $20, $50, and $100. Larger denominations are not in general circulation. All notes are the same size and the same black-and-green color, so be sure to double-check your cash before you dispense it.

Coins: 1¢ (penny), 5¢ (nickel), 10¢ (dime), 25¢ (quarter), 50¢ (half dollar), and $1.

Banks and currency exchange. Banks are open from 9am to 5pm, Monday to Thursday, until 6pm Friday, and some operate on Saturday morning as well. You can change foreign currency at the airport, at leading banks downtown, and at bureaux de change in areas frequented by tourists or financiers.

Credit cards. When buying something or paying a restaurant bill you may be asked, "Cash or charge?" In the US "plastic" money is a way of life. Most Americans carry a variety of credit cards, and they are accepted in most places. But you may be asked for supplementary identification.

Traveler's checks. Banks, stores, restaurants, and hotels almost universally accept dollar-denominated traveler's checks as the equivalent of cash. It's straightforward if the checks are issued by American Express or an American bank, much less so if the issuer is not well known in the US. If your traveler's checks are in foreign denominations, they can be changed only in banks with experience in international transactions. Exchange only small amounts at a time, keeping the balance in your hotel safe if possible. Keep a record of the serial number of each check in a separate place to facilitate a refund in the event of loss or theft.

Sales taxes. In the absence of VAT, cities and states around the US levy sales taxes and other hidden extras. An 8½ percent sales tax is added to the price of all goods and services in San Francisco.

O

OPENING HOURS

Shops. Department stores are generally open from Monday to Saturday between 9.30 and 10am and stay in business until 6pm or, in some cases, as late as 8pm. They are often open on Sunday.

Museums. Hours vary, but 10am to 5pm is your best bet; Monday is the favorite closing day, and some also close on Tuesday.

Banks. Hours are generally from 9am to 4pm Monday to Friday, though some stay open longer.

Post offices. Branch post offices stay open from 8:30 or 9am to 5 or 5:30pm Monday to Friday; the General Post Office is open round the clock.

P

PLANNING YOUR TRIP on the WEB

These web sites are full of information to aid in getting a head start on your vacation.

www.bayarea.citysearch.com A comprehensive, regularly updated site devoted to all things San Francisco including arts, entertainment, dining, and attractions with links to the hotel reservation network.

www.sfbg.com The San Francisco Bay Guardian site with event listings and the low-down on nightlife.

www.sfgate.com The *San Francisco Chronicle* web site. Read all about it.

www.qsanfrancisco.com A web site for gay and lesbian travelers.

www.sfweekly.com Catering to young urbanites, *SF Weekly*'s site has complete entertainment listings.

www.sfstation Entertainment, restaurant, arts, and events listings. Very thorough and cutting edge.

POLICE

The blue-uniformed city police, some of them multilingual, are courteous and helpful to tourists. Imitating a feature of Japanese life, they operate *kobans* or mini police stations at Market and Powell streets; in Chinatown on Grant Avenue between Washington and Jackson streets; and in Japantown at Post and Buchanan streets. Out of town on roads, you'll encounter the California Highway Patrol in tan uniforms with ranger hats. In an emergency dial **911.**

POST OFFICES

The US postal service deals only with mail. The main post office is at Seventh Street and Mission Street. A branch post office in the basement of Macy's department store, Union Square, is convenient.

PUBLIC TRANSPORTATION

Muni Metro **streetcars** operate underground in the downtown district, above ground beyond the center. There are five lines, making the same Market Street stops as the BART system. Board buses through the front door and leave from the rear. The exact fare is required; drivers don't give change. The problem is avoided if you buy a Muni Passport valid for a full day (or three days or a week) on all lines, including the cable cars. The passes, on sale at the Visitor Information Center *(see page 122)* and other locations, also provide discounts to museums and other attractions.

Cable cars, on three lines, go over the hills to the principal areas of tourist interest. Tickets are sold on board and drivers will make change. The cable cars are usually crowded, mostly with tourists enjoying the invigorating ride. Never board or leave a cable car until it has stopped; get off facing the direction of travel.

BART, the pioneering Bay Area Rapid Transit system, offers fast, quiet, comfortable rail service between San Francisco and 25 stations in the East Bay area (Oakland, Richmond, and so forth). Maps and charts in the stations explain the routes and the computerized ticketing system. There are change-giving machines alongside the coin-operated ticket dispensing machines.

Intercity buses operate from the Transbay Terminal, at First and Mission streets. AC Transit crosses the Bay Bridge to Berkeley, Oakland, and other East Bay communities. Golden Gate Transit uses the Golden Gate Bridge to serve Marin and Sonoma Counties. Samtrans is the San Mateo County service, going as far as Palo Alto.

Taxis are usually plentiful. They congregate at the luxury hotels but you can hail one in the street. If you're staying at an out-of-the-way location, it's convenient to telephone for a radio-dispatched taxi.

Ferry boats seemed to be doomed when the bridges were built but today they once more provide commuter service and useful tourist travel. The principal terminals are the Ferry Building, at the foot of Market Street, and Piers 39 to 41/2. The Blue & Gold Fleet, which does big business in Bay sightseeing cruises, also goes to Oakland, Alameda, and Alcatraz. Golden Gate Ferries go to Sausalito and Larkspur. The Red & White Fleet cruises to Sausalito, Tiburon, and Vallejo.

R

RELIGION

Every religious denomination has a house of worship in San Francisco. The Saturday newspapers list times of some of the services. The Visitor Information Center *(see page 122)* has a list of church addresses. For a rousing, gospel music-filled Sunday serviceshow up a half-hour before the 9am or 11am celebration at Glide Memorial Church, 330 Ellis Street (Tel: 415-771-6300).

S

SMOKING

Smoking is prohibited in public places such as office buildings, schools, libraries, public rest rooms, and service or check-out lines. In liberal San Francisco, it's even banned in bars and restaurants. Domestic airlines prohibit smoking on-board planes.

T

TELEPHONE

The American telephone system is run by private, regional companies. Coin- or card-operated phones are found in all public places — hotel lobbies, drugstores, gas stations, bars, restaurants, and along the streets. Directions for use are clearly stated on the machine. For local directory assistance dial 411 or 555-1212 (free of charge). When calling long distance, the rules of competition mean that you often have to choose between companies by pushing one or another button; to the visitor it scarcely matters which. Evening (after 5pm) and weekend rates are much cheaper. Many hotels, airlines, and business firms have toll free numbers (beginning 800, 888, or 877) so you can avoid long-distance charges.

Some hotels add a hefty surcharge to their guests' outgoing calls, local or long-distance. If it seems exorbitant you can go out to use a pay phone. But you'll have to have a hoard of coins at the ready; an electronic voice may break in to tell you to insert more. However, phone cards and sometimes credit cards may now also be used for dialing telephone calls.

The long distance code for the city of San Francisco is 415. The code for most of the East Bay area, including Oakland and Berkeley, is 510, and 650 is the area code for the peninsula (south of San Francisco).

TIME ZONES

The continental United States is divided into four time zones. San Francisco is in the Pacific zone, which is 8 hours behind GMT.

San Francisco

Between the first Sunday in April and the last Sunday in October, the clock is advanced 1 hour for Daylight Saving Time (GMT minus 7 hours). These dates are not quite synchronized with the changes in other countries. The following chart shows the time in various cities when it is noon in San Francisco.

San Francisco	Chicago	New York	London	Paris
noon	2pm	3pm	8pm	9pm

TIPPING

You are expected to add about 15–20 percent to restaurant and bar bills, based on the total of the bill. If service has been exceptionally good, 20–25 percent is appropriate. Even in informal coffee shops, some coins are often left on the table or counter. Cinema or theater ushers are not tipped, but doormen, cloakroom attendants, etc., should be remunerated – no less than 50 cents. Some guidelines:

Bartender	$1 per drink
Porter	$1 per bag
Hotel maid	$1 per day (except for very short stays)
Lavatory attendant	50¢
Taxi driver	about 15 percent
Tour guide	10–15 percent
Hairdresser/barber	15 percent

TOILETS

Some dark-green coin-operated public bathrooms are located near tourist sites on Market Street and Fisherman's Wharf. Many restaurants discourage anyone but patrons from using their facilities; your best bet is to try a department store, hotel, or gas station.

TOURIST INFORMATION

For advance inquiries, write to the San Francisco Convention & Visitors Bureau, 201 Third Street, Suite 900, San Francisco, CA

94103. The bureau offers a variety of information kits available on their website; most packages are free. You could also contact the US Embassy, Visit USA Committee, or USTTA (United States Travel and Tourism Administration) in your own country:

Australia: Suite 6106, MLC Center, King and Castlereagh Streets, Sydney, New South Wales 2000; Tel: (612) 233 4666

Canada: 800 Rochester Boulevard, West Suite 1110, Montreal, Quebec H3B 1X9; Tel: (514) 861 5036

Ireland: Irish Visit USA Committee, c/o Tour America, 62 Middle Abbey St., Dublin; Tel: (353) (1) 662-0860.

New Zealand: Visit USA Commitee, 129A Kohimarama Road, Kohimarama, Auckland; Tel: (64) (9) 528 4447.

South Africa: US Embassy, P.O. Box 9536, Pretoria 0001; Tel: (271) (2) 342-1048

UK: 22 Sackville Street, London W1X 2EA; Tel: 020 7439 7433

San Francisco's Visitor Information Center <www.sfvisitor.org> is located on the lower level of Hallidie Plaza at Market and Powell streets, near the cable car terminus. The office is open weekdays 9am–5pm, Saturday and Sunday 9am–3pm. Telephone inquiries: (415) 391-2000. A recorded message listing daily events is available on (415) 391-2001. (In French, 415-391-2003; German, 415-391-2004; Spanish, 415-391-2122; Japanese, 415-391-2101.)

WEIGHTS & MEASURES

Efforts to ease the United States into the metric system are proceeding slowly. The government itself is said to be converting to international measurements, and indeed the national parks use kilometers, but in real life it's still inches, feet, yards, miles, and degrees Fahrenheit.

Length

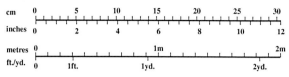

Weight

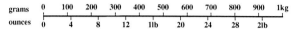

Temperature

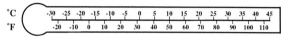

Y

YOUTH HOSTELS

The Golden Gate Council of American Youth Hostels operates budget accommodation at Union Square and Fort Mason as well as hostels in scenic locations around the Bay area. The address of the Union Square installation, with lodgings for 175 people, is 312 Mason Street, San Francisco, CA 94102; Tel: (415) 788-5604. You can contact the Fort Mason Hostel, capacity 150, at Building 240, Fort Mason, San Francisco, CA 94123; Tel: (415) 771-7277. In Sausalito, you can try the Golden Gate Youth Hostel, 941 Fort Barry, Sausalito, CA 94965; Tel: (415) 331-2777. Additional hostels are listed in the Lodging Guide issued by the San Francisco Convention & Visitors Bureau *(see page 122)*.

Note that advance booking is essential at all Youth Hostels in San Francisco. For more information, contact: the American Youth Hostels Inc, National Offices, PO Box 37613, Washington, DC 20013–7613; Tel: (202) 783-6171.

Recommended Hotels

San Francisco holds a dizzying array of hotels, motels, Bed & Breakfasts, and inns that range from dull to dramatic. All the major chains are well represented, but the more interesting rooms are located in "boutique" hotels. These are small properties developed around a theme, such as books, rock and roll, or the movies, that gives the hotel some definable personality.

Whether a boutique, a B&B, or a 1,000-room behemoth that will honor your frequent flier mileage, all the hotels listed below are well-scrubbed and offer excellent service. Rooms will generally include cable television and direct-dial telephones, but not air-conditioning (it isn't really necessary). If there is no concierge, desk clerks will do their best to provide information and make tour and restaurant reservations. Since San Francisco is a very popular convention and tourist town, it is imperative to make reservations well ahead of time. If you haven't done so, phone SF Reservations, Tel: (800) 677-1500 (toll-free in US) or 415-227-1500.

The stars below refer to high-season rack rates for a standard double room, exclusive of taxes (14 percent). Prices do not include parking or breakfast unless noted. When making reservations at the larger hotels, always inquire about special packages and discounts. Toll-free numbers are effective only within North America.

The following symbols apply for a double room:

$$$$$	above $250
$$$$	$200–$250
$$$	$150–$200
$$	$125–$150
$	below $125

San Francisco

UNION SQUARE

Andrews Hotel $$ *624 Post Street, SF 94108; Tel: (415) 563-6877; (800) 926-3739 (toll-free in US); fax: (415) 928-6919; web site <www.andrewshotel.com>.* A 1905 Victorian well-located two blocks west of Union Square. The rooms and baths are on the small side, but rates include a continental breakfast and evening wine reception. Smoking is not allowed.

Campton Place Hotel $$$$$ *340 Stockton Street, SF 94108; Tel: (415) 781-5555; (800) 235-4300 (toll-free in US); fax: (415) 955-5536; web site <www.camptonplace.com>.* Elegant, luxurious, and intimate, this is one of the most renowned and refined hotels in the city. The service is excellent, the amenities are top-notch, and the hotel restaurant consistently merits top ratings. Wheelchair accessible.

Cartwright Hotel $$–$$$ *524 Sutter Street, SF 94102; Tel: (415) 421-2865; (800) 794-7661 (toll-free in US); fax: (415) 398-6345; web site <www.cartwrighthotel.com>.* This genteel hotel has tastefully decorated rooms and many amenities. A continental breakfast and afternoon tea are included. Five suites are available, a plus for families, and two floors are reserved for smokers. Be sure to ask about specials.

Chancellor Hotel $$ *433 Powell Street, SF 94102; Tel: (415) 362-2004; (800) 428-4748 (toll-free in US); fax: (415) 362-1403; web site <www.chancellorhotel.com>.* The same family has owned and managed this charming hotel since 1917, which is on the Powell Street cable car line and within a stone's throw of the major department stores around Union Square. Rooms are comfortably furnished; baths are small but well-stocked.

Commodore International $-$$ *825 Sutter Street, SF 94109; Tel: (415) 923-6800; (800) 338-6848 (toll-free in US); fax: (415) 923-6804; web site <www.sftrips.com>.* Spacious rooms are bright and recently renovated in a nautical theme. The location is a bit close to the seedy Tenderloin neighborhood for some, but that's why rates are low. A café sits on one side of the property and a trendy bar is on the other.

Golden Gate Hotel $ *775 Bush Street, SF 94108; Tel: (415) 392-3702; (800) 835-1118 (toll-free in US); fax: (415) 392-6202; web site <www.goldengatehotel.com>.* A cozy family-run hotel near Union Square and two blocks from the Chinatown Gate. The pretty rooms contain few amenities, but rates include a continental breakfast and afternoon tea. Smoking is not allowed in the hotel: Some rooms with private bath.

Handlery Union Square Hotel $$$ *351 Geary Street, SF 94102; Tel: (415) 781-7800, (800) 843-4343 (toll-free in US); fax: (415) 781-0269; web site <www.handlerysf@handlery.com>.* A good choice for families, the hotel has a heated pool, morning and evening room service, even Nintendo games. Club rooms, located in an adjacent building, are large and offer dressing areas, robes, newspapers, and fresh decor. Wheelchair accessible.

The Inn at Union Square $$$-$$$$$ *440 Post Street, SF 94102; Tel: (415) 397-3510; (800) 288-4346 (toll-free in US); fax: (415) 989-0529; web site <www.unionsquare.com>.* Furnished with Georgian antiques, this is a "European-style" inn with excellent service and a no-tipping policy. Extras include a complimentary continental breakfast, afternoon tea, fresh flowers, newspapers, and concierge. Smoking, however, is not allowed in the hotel: Wheelchair accessible.

San Francisco

The Juliana $$$ *590 Bush Street, SF 94108; Tel: (415) 392-2540; (800) 328-3880 (toll-free in US); fax: (415) 391-8447; web site <www.julianahotel.com>.* Situated between Nob Hill and Union Square, the Juliana is a cozy retreat with gaily decorated rooms and suites that include coffee pots, irons, and hair dryers. An evening wine reception is hosted nightly; continental breakfast is available for an extra charge.

Kensington Park Hotel $$$ *450 Post Street, SF 94102; Tel: (415) 788-6400; (800) 553-1900 (toll-free in US); fax: (415) 399-9484; web site <www.personalityhotels.com>.* Large, recently renovated rooms and baths distinguish this fine hotel, which is next door to a trendy seafood restaurant and shares space with a live theater. Rates include continental breakfast and afternoon tea; concierge services are friendly and helpful.

King George Hotel $$–$$$ *334 Mason Street, SF 94102; Tel: (415) 781-5050; (800) 288-6005 (toll-free in US). web site <www.kinggeorge.com>.* Opened in 1913, this is a British-themed hotel with small rooms and baths updated in 1998. 24-hour room service is available plus a tea room presided over by a handsome portrait of Queen Elizabeth. Continental breakfast and afternoon tea are served daily, but aren't included in the rates.

The Maxwell $$$–$$$$ *386 Geary Street, SF 94102; Tel: (415) 986-2000; (888) 734-6299 (toll-free in US); fax: (415) 397-2447; web site <www.sftrips.com>.* An inviting, theatrical lobby leads to Art-Deco–inspired guestrooms that range from small to spacious. Amenities include a newsletter highlighting shopping opportunities around the city. Desk staff provide concierge services.

Hotel Monaco $$$$ *501 Geary Street, SF 94102; Tel: (415) 292-0100; (866) 622-5284 (toll-free in US); fax: (415) 292-0111; web site <www.hotelmonaco.com>.* Rooms in this hotel are comfortable and plush, featuring lots of wallpaper, patterns, canopied beds, and modern furniture with a 1920s-inspired twist. Major amenities include a fitness room. The excellent Grand Café is next door and provides 24-hour room service. Wheelchair accessible.

Petite Auberge $$–$$$ *863 Bush Street, SF 94102; Tel: (415) 928-6000; (800) 365-3004 (toll-free in US); fax: (415) 673-7214; web site <www.foursisters.com>.* A very Romantic B&B, with a full breakfast served in a homey dining room as well as complimentary afternoon tea and wine. The less expensive rooms have showers only; the high-end rooms are large with full baths, and all are very comfortable. Book ahead.

Hotel Rex $$$–$$$$$ *562 Sutter Street, SF 94102; Tel: (415) 433-4434; (800) 433-4434 (toll-free in US); fax: (415) 433-3695; web site <sftrips.com>.* With a nod to the 1930s, the sophisticated Rex is a favorite among the literati. There's even an antiquarian bookstore on the premises. An evening wine hour is complimentary; a continental breakfast is available at an additional charge.

The Ritz-Carlton, San Francisco $$$$$ *600 Stockton Street, SF 94108; Tel: (415) 296-7465; (800) 241-3333 (toll-free in US); fax: (415) 291-0288; web site <www.ritzcarlton.com>.* Once a giant neo-classical corporate headquarters, now a luxury hotel catering to deep pocketbooks. Opened in 1991, the Ritz offers enormous rooms, a fitness center, indoor pool, fine dining restaurant, and primo service. Wheelchair accessible.

Sir Francis Drake $$$-$$$$$ *450 Powell Street, SF 94102; Tel: (415) 392-7755; (800) 795-7129 (toll-free in US); fax: (415) 391-8719; web site <www.sirfrancisdrake.com>.* Glide past the uniformed valets into the grand lobby of this 1928 landmark building. The excellent Scala's Bistro is located next door and there's a small fitness room and popular nightclub on the premises. Wheelchair accessible.

Hotel Triton $$$-$$$$ *342 Grant Avenue, SF 94108; Tel: (415) 394-0500; (800) 800-1299 (toll-free in US); fax: (415) 394-0555; web site <www.hotel-tritonsf.com>.* Rock music greets patrons entering this trendy hotel just across the street from the Chinatown Dragon Gate. The wild designs and mod furniture scattered around the lobby are amusing, but don't compensate for the tiny bedrooms. Lots of amenities, including robes, hair dryers, concierge.

Warwick Regis $$-$$$ *490 Geary Street, SF 94102; Tel: (415) 928-7900; (800) 827-3447 (toll-free in US); fax: (415) 441-8788; web site <www.warwickhotels.com>.* Guests receive all the amenities expected of a much larger hotel—twice-daily maid service, fresh flowers, marble-tiled baths, and 24-hour room service—for a relatively modest tariff. All the elegantly appointed guestrooms are quiet. The Union Square location is especially convenient for theater-goers.

Westin St Francis $$$$ *335 Powell Street, SF 94102; Tel: (415) 397-7000; (800) 228-3000 (toll-free in US); fax: (415) 774-0124; web site <www.westin.com>.* The location, across the street from Union Square, adds to the excitement of staying at this legendary hotel: If the historic aspects interest you, reserve a room in the original building. Baths are small and guest rooms rather dark, but they're furnished with handsome reproductions and chandeliers. On-site fitness center, room service, and restaurants complete the package. Wheelchair accessible.

The York Hotel $–$$$ *940 Sutter Street, SF, 94109; Tel: (415) 885-6800; (800) 808-YORK; fax: (415) 885-2115; web site <www.yorkhotel.com>.* The setting for Hitchcock's *Vertigo* has recently been renovated and offers a deluxe continental breakfast with the very reasonably-priced room rates. The Plush Room theater, once a prohibition-era speakeasy now known for torch singers and cabaret, is located here.

NOB HILL

Huntington Hotel $$$$$ *1075 California Street, SF 94108; Tel: (415) 474-5400; (800) 227-4683 (toll-free in US); fax: (415) 474-6227; web site <www.slh.com>.* A refined family-owned hotel built in 1924 at the top of Nob Hill, where publicity-shy celebrities stay in discreet luxury. Originally an apartment building, rooms are larger than average. For views, ask for a room above the eighth floor. A park and playground is located across the street, making the location especially pleasant for families with young children. Wheelchair accessible.

Mark Hopkins Inter-Continental $$$$$ *999 California, SF 94108; Tel: (415) 392-3434; (800) 327-0200 (toll-free in US); web site <www.sanfranciscointerconti.com>.* At the summit of Nob Hill, with grand views in all directions, this hotel offers totally redecorated luxury rooms on the site of the original Mark Hopkins mansion. The rooftop cocktail lounge, Top of the Mark, has been a city tradition since 1939, and an atmosphere of quiet refinement prevails throughout. Wheelchair accessible.

Nob Hill Lambourne $$$$–$$$$$ *725 Pine Street, SF 94108; Tel: (415) 433-2287; (800) 274-8466 (toll-free in US); fax: (415) 433-0975; web site <www.nobhilllambourne.com>.* Intimate and soothing, with spacious guestrooms with compact kitchenettes. Desk staff can schedule on-site massages and spa treatments. A continental breakfast is included in the rates.

THE EMBARCADERO

Embarcadero Hyatt $$$–$$$$$ *5 Market Street, SF 94105; Tel: (415) 788-1234; toll-free (800) 233-1234; fax: (415) 398-2567; web site <www.sanfrancisco.regency.hyatt.com>.* The location at the foot of Market Street is good for walkers and public transportation. Some great restaurants are close by. Big rooms, on-site fitness center, the works. Wheelchair accessible.

Harbor Court Hotel $$$$ *165 Steuart Street, SF 94105; Tel: (415) 882-1300; (866) 792-6283 (toll-free in US); fax: (415) 882-1313; web site <www.harborcourthotel.com>.* Across from the Rincon Center, this 1907 building with bay views has been converted into a "European-style" hotel with comfortable rooms and varied luxury amenities. Guests have complimentary access to the state-of-the-art YMCA next door. Wheelchair accessible.

SOMA

Hotel Milano $$$–$$$$ *55 Fifth Street, SF, 94103; Tel: (415) 543-8555; (800) 398-7555 (toll-free in US); fax: (415) 543-5885; web site <www.hotelmilano.citysearch.com>.* The location – next door to the San Francisco Centre, a few blocks from Yerba Buena Gardens, and close to an underground Muni station – makes this hotel a good pick for energetic tourists who like to shop. An on-site fitness room, restaurant, and full service make up for the spare decor. Wheelchair accessible.

MARINA

Hotel Del Sol $$ *3100 Webster Street, SF 94123; Tel: (415) 921-5520; (877) 433-5765 (toll-free in US); fax: (415) 931-4137; web site <www.sftrips.com>.* Once a boring, ordinary motel, the Del Sol has had a radical make-over and now proves that looks are almost everything. Color is used to great effect, splashed on walls, fabrics, and mosaic tiles that decorate tabletops and walkways. Comfortable medium- to large-sized rooms surround a heated swimming pool, small lawn and hammock; suites are available, and parking is free. Wheelchair accessible.

The Marina Inn $ *3110 Octavia, SF 94123; Tel: (415) 928-1000; (800) 274-1420 (toll-free in US); fax: (415) 928-5909; web site <www.marinainn.com>.* This is an inexpensive, gracious Victorian inn off Lombard Street, not far from the Golden Gate Bridge, the Presidio, and the upscale shopping on Union and Chestnut streets. The rooms are simply furnished; inside rooms are considerably quieter but don't have much natural light. A Continental breakfast is included in the price. Wheelchair accessible.

NORTH BEACH/FISHERMAN'S WHARF

Hotel Bohème $$ *444 Columbus Street, SF 94133; Tel: (415) 433-9111; fax: (415) 362-6292; web site <www.hotel boheme.com>.* A flight of narrow stairs brings you inside this delightful small hotel situated in the heart of North Beach. Iron beds and brightly painted walls grace the small but lovely bedrooms, and the baths are well-stocked with toiletries. The front desk stagg are happy to assist with rental cars, dinner reservations, and tours.

Tuscan Inn $$$ *425 North Point, SF 94133; Tel: (415) 561-1100; (800) 648-4626 (toll-free in US); fax: (415) 561-1199; web site <www.tuscaninn.com>.* Of the many hotels around Fisherman's Wharf, this is by far the most pleasant. The concierge is enthusiastic and helpful, the attractive rooms are well-sized by local standards, and the location is appealing to families who wish, to be near Pier 39. Wheelchair accessible.

WESTERN ADDITION (ALAMO SQUARE)

The Archbishop's Mansion $$-$$$$$ *1000 Fulton Street, San Francisco CA 94117; Tel: (415) 563-7872; (800) 543-5820 (toll free in the US); fax: (415) 885-3193; web site <www.thearchbishopsmansion.com>.* This exquisite, French chateau mansion in Alamo Square was built in 1904 for the archbishop of San Francisco and is a historical landmark. A full breakfast is served in the sumptuous dining room or delivered to rooms.

HAIGHT-ASHBURY

The Red Victorian Bed & Breakfast Inn $-$$ *1665 Haight Street, SF94117; Tel: (415) 864-1978; fax: (415) 863-3293; web site <www.redvic.com>.* The Summer of Love is alive and well at this peace haven on Haight Street. Reasonably-priced '60s-themed rooms have private baths, canopied beds, colorful quilts and tie-dyed fabrics. No televisions but plenty of good vibes.

The Stanyan Park Hotel $$-$$$ *750 Stanyan Street, San Francisco, 94117; Tel: (415) 751-1000; fax: (415) 668-5454; web site <www.stanyanpark.com>.* An elegant, affordable early 20th century boutique hotel located across the street from Golden Gate Park. Suites are large and ideal for families. Continental breakfast included.

Recommended Restaurants

With over 3,300 restaurants in the city limits, there are many worthy dining establishments from which to choose; the ones below provide a representative sample of neighborhoods, styles of cuisine, and prices. Always phone ahead for dinner reservations; you're competing with San Francisco's resident population of gourmets, who have made table-hopping an art form. The following three price categories apply for a three-course meal without wine:

$$$	Over $40
$$	$20–$40
$	under $20

Remember, taxes (8.5 percent) and tips (15 percent) will also increase your bill.

CHINATOWN

Kay Cheung $ *615 Jackson Street; Tel: (415) 989-6838.* Open daily for dim sum, lunch and dinner. This small, pleasant dining room serves delicious Hong Kong–style Chinese dishes at a great price. Interesting selection of fresh seafood (plucked live from tanks) and dim sum. If you end up sharing a table, take an opportunity to learn about dumplings from the Chinatown regulars who come here in-between shopping excursions. Major credit cards.

R&G Lounge $ *631 Kearney Street; Tel: (415) 982-7877.* Open for lunch and dinner daily. Downstairs you'll find excellent Hong Kong Chinese food served in a drab setting by bored waiters. The upstairs dining room is much more comfortable with attentive servers who can help design your meal. No matter where they seat you, don't pass up the live spot shrimp cooked two ways. Major credit cards.

UNION SQUARE

Dottie's True Blue Café $ *522 Jones Street; Tel: (415) 885-2767.* Open for breakfast and lunch Wednesday through Sunday only. If you like a big breakfast featuring fresh baked goods, pancakes, omelets, and maybe a pork chop, get in line for one of the 11 tables packed into this tiny place. Lunch isn't quite as crowded, but it's equally good. Major credit cards.

Grand Café $$ *501 Geary Street; Tel: (415) 292-0101.* Open daily for breakfast, lunch, and dinner. There's always a buzz of activity inside this vast muralled restaurant. It's a destination for tourists as well as locals looking for a major meal or just an after-theater bite. Roasts, fresh fish, brick-oven pizzas, big desserts – every plate receives careful attention from the kitchen. Major credit cards.

Le Colonial $$$ *20 Cosmo Place; Tel: (415) 931-3600.* Open weekdays for lunch; dinner nightly. Flavorful French-Vietnamese food is formally proffered in a dining room replete with rattan, pressed tin, potted palms, and ceiling fans. The upstairs lounge is a great place for a drink and to listen to live jazz on Friday and Sunday nights. Major credit cards.

Scala's Bistro $$ *432 Powell Street; Tel: (415) 395-8555.* Open daily for breakfast, lunch, and dinner. Next to the Sir Francis Drake hotel, this Italian restaurant has a broad menu, comfort-able booths, and a warm, clubby atmosphere. Highlights include a terrific Caesar salad and well-prepared fish. Major credit cards.

Vino $ *701 Union Street; Tel: (415) 392-8466*. Ample, affordable and healthy family-style meals a short walk from Washington Square Park. If you're looking for fresh, flavorful Italian/Mediterranean cuisine without heavy sauces and hefty prices, look no further.

NOB HILL

Charles Nob Hill $$$ *1250 Jones Street; Tel: (415) 771-5400*. Open for dinner only, Tuesday through Sunday. Ron Siegal, the resident kitchen god at this elegant and refined restaurant, is renowned in culinary circles for taking on Japan television's *Iron Chef* – and winning. His contemporary American cuisine is exquisitely prepared and presented with a slight French flair. The short rib ravioli underneath a perfect filet mignon is an especially magnificent dish. Major credit cards.

EMBARCADERO/FINANCIAL DISTRICT

Kokkari $$$ *200 Jackson Street; Tel: (415) 981 0983*. Open weekdays for lunch; dinner Monday through Saturday. An Aristotle Onassis–sort of Greek taverna with beamed ceilings, a massive fireplace, Oriental carpets, and huge dishes of rich food. (Don't expect to see anyone intentionally smash a plate.) The crowd exudes a robust sense of well-being. Reservations are advised. Major credit cards.

Plouf $$ *40 Belden Place; Tel: (415) 986-6491*. Open for lunch and dinner Monday through Saturday. There are a number of good cafés with outdoor seating on Belden Place, an alley off Bush and Kearney streets near the Financial District. Plouf specializes in delicious seafood prepared with a French affect and the waiters also give the impression you've arrived in the Paris of the west. Major credit cards.

Tadich Grill $$ *240 California Street; Tel: (415) 392-1849.*
Open for lunch and dinner Monday through Saturday. This the
oldest continually operating restaurant in California, with wood-
en booths, white linen, and waiters as crusty as the sourdough.
The menu of classics, including lobster Newburg, is printed
daily. The cognoscenti order whatever fresh fish is available,
grilled. Major credit cards.

SOMA

Hawthorne Lane $$$ *22 Hawthorne Lane (at Howard); Tel:
(415) 777-9779.* Open for lunch weekdays and dinner nightly.
The chefs who opened Postrio departed a few years back to open
their own fine-dining establishment with a California/Asian-
influenced cuisine. The art-filled setting and the food (for example, roasted local lamb with garlic chive risotto and a warm snap
pea and water chestnut salad) are quite elegant, but overall it's
warm and accessible. Major credit cards.

Thirsty Bear Brewing Company $$ *661 Howard Street; Tel:
(415) 974-0905.* Open for lunch Monday through Saturday; din-
ner nightly. Excellent house-made beers and outstanding
Catalan food have made this spot a favorite. The fish cheeks are
one of the great *tapas* offered, but save room for a Sagrada
Familia, two upside-down wafer cones filled with chocolate
mousse and decorated with whipped cream. Major credit cards.

NORTH BEACH

Enrico's Sidewalk Café $$ *504 Broadway; Tel: (415) 982-
6223.* Open for lunch and dinner daily. It's always fun to dine on
the patio here and watch the action along busy and bawdy
Broadway. Along with a seasonal menu of California cuisine,
there's live jazz and a convivial atmosphere. Major credit cards.

Juicey Lucy $ *703 Columbus Avenue; Tel: (415) 786-1285.* A groovy café and organic juice bar where good vibes abound. Healthy and tasty lunch options include organic salads, vegan specialties, and veggie sandwiches.

L'Osteria del Forno $ *519 Columbus Avenue; Tel: (415) 982-1124.* Open for lunch and dinner Wednesday through Monday. For casual but satisfying Italian food including marvelous antipasti, thin-crusted pizzas, a daily pasta dish, and a fine roast pork loin simmered in a milky broth. A kid pleaser as well. Cash only.

CIVIC CENTER/HAYES VALLEY

Hayes Street Grill $$ *320 Hayes Street; Tel: (415) 863-5545.* Open for lunch weekdays; dinner nightly. Practically a local institution, this restaurant features fresh seafood prepared simply, with integrity, and served with terrific french fries. Non-fish items, such as a juicy hamburger, are also wonderful. Local politicians eat lunch here; the pre-symphony, opera, and ballet crowd fill the tables before 8pm. Major credit cards.

Zuni Café $$$ *1658 Market Street (Civic Center); Tel: (415) 552-2522.* Open for lunch Tuesday through Saturday; dinner Tuesday through Sunday; Sunday brunch. Make reservations and elbow your way past the crowded copper bar for the best roasted chicken and bread salad for two imaginable. Actually, everything on the California-cuisine based menu is going to be great. Major credit cards.

CASTRO

Chow $ *215 Church Street; Tel: (415) 552-2469.* Open daily for lunch and dinner. For casual but well-prepared meals that will appeal to children and grown-ups, make your way to this popular place or their equally busy restaurant on 9th Avenue by Golden Gate Park. Terrific pizzas, salads, sandwiches, brick-oven roasted chicken, and daily specials at prices that'll amaze you. Major credit cards.

JAPANTOWN

Café Kati $$$ *1963 Sutter Street; Tel: (415) 775-7313.* Open for dinner Tuesday through Sunday. Another outstanding neighborhood restaurant with a legion of loyal followers, this is well worth a cab ride out of Union Square. Major credit cards.

Mifune $ *1737 Post Street; Tel: (415) 922-0337.* The San Francisco branch of a famous Osaka restaurant proposes Japanese *udon* and *soba* in all their forms, often in steaming soups. This is the place for a quick lunch or dinner, and kids are very happy in the midst of all these noodles. Major credit cards.

MARINA

Greens $$–$$$ *Building A, Fort Mason; Tel: (415) 771-6222.* Open for lunch Tuesday through Saturday, dinner Monday through Saturday, and Sunday brunch. In a one-time army warehouse on the bay, an airy up-market vegetarian restaurant that even carnivores rave about. The Saturday evening prix fixe is a relative bargain and comes with lovely bay views. Reservations are essential. Major credit cards.

THE MISSION DISTRICT

Delfina $$ *3621 18th Street; Tel: (415) 552-4055.* Open nightly for dinner. The kitchen in this storefront restaurant turns out delicious Tuscan Italian food that provides a star turn for local, seasonal produce, fish, and meat. (If sea bass happens to be on the menu, catch it.) Reservations are essential as this is a favorite neighborhood pick among residents from all over the city. Major credit cards.

OUTSIDE THE CITY

Oakland

Bay Wolf Café $$–$$$ *3853 Piedmont Avenue, Oakland; Tel: (510) 655-6004.* Open for lunch Monday through Friday and dinner nightly. A pioneer of California-style nouvelle cuisine maintains enviable quality. Keenly chosen wine list. Major credit cards.

Yoshi's $$ *510 Embarcadero West, Jack London Square, Oakland; Tel: (510) 238-9200.* Open daily for lunch and dinner. The large, brightly lit restaurant serves good, if predictable, Japanese food and has a lively sushi bar. Diners receive priority seating in the well-known jazz club. Major credit cards.

Berkeley

Chez Panisse $$–$$$ *1517 Shattuck Avenue, Berkeley; Tel: (510) 548-5525.* Open Monday through Saturday for dinner; the café is also open for lunch. A redwood cottage is the shrine for spectacularly tasty and original California cuisine. The upstairs café, which does not require reservations, is less expensive than the downstairs dining room for which reservations are essential. Major credit cards.

Marin

Guaymas $$–$$$ *5 Main Street, Tiburon; Tel: (415) 435-6300.* Open daily for lunch and dinner. Modern Mexican decor and cuisine combines with panoramas of San Francisco. A major hangout for tourists. Major credit cards.

Lark Creek Inn $$$ *234 Magnolia Avenue, Larkspur; Tel: (415) 924-7766.* Open for lunch weekdays, dinner nightly, Sunday brunch. Set among a few redwoods in the pretty town of Larkspur, you'll be treated to top-notch American cuisine from the best hamburger in the state to a smoky, sun-dried tomato and ham hock–filled ravoli. Great children's menu. Reservations advised. Major credit cards.

Wine Country

Bistro Jeanty $$ *6510 Washington Street, Yountville; Tel: (707) 944-0103.* Open for lunch and dinner daily. A fairly new, very French bistro with an outdoor patio and spirited inside dining room and bar. The seasonal menu of homey dishes (coq au vin, rabbit and sweetbread ragout, cassoulet, a simple steak frites) is so satisfying you want to eat here again and again. Major credit cards.

Martini House $$$ *1245 Spring Street, St. Helena (Napa Valley); Tel: (707) 963-2233.* A two-story bungalow with rustic yet genteel décor, and top-notch seasonal Californian cuisine for those with an adventurous palate. For the ultimate taste sensation try the chef's tasting menu paired with wine.

Tra Vigne $$$ *1050 Charter Oak Avenue, St. Helena; Tel: (707) 963-4444.* Open daily for lunch and dinner. A large airy dining room opens onto a vine-filled patio with formidable stone tables and a whimsical fountain. The Italian fare is based on what's currently in the markets, and if it's tomato season, don't miss the fruits paired with fresh mozzarella. A delicatessen, the Cantinetta, offers prepared foods for picnicking. Major credit cards.

INDEX

BIRDS of
CO

Susan C L

Photographs by Michael and Patricia Fogden

B L O O M S B U R Y
LONDON • NEW DELHI • NEW YORK • SYDNEY

Bloomsbury Natural History
An imprint of Bloomsbury Publishing Plc

50 Bedford Square
London
WC1B 3DP
UK

1385 Broadway
New York
NY 10018
USA

www.bloomsbury.com

BLOOMSBURY and the Diana logo are trademarks of
Bloomsbury Publishing Plc

First published by New Holland UK Ltd, 2005 as
A Photographic Guide to the Birds of Costa Rica
This edition first published by Bloomsbury, 2016

© Bloomsbury Publishing Plc, 2016
© text Susan Fogden 2016
© photographs Michael and Patricia Fogden 2016

British Library Cataloguing-in-Publication Data
A catalogue record for this book is available from the British Library.

Library of Congress Cataloguing-in-Publication data has been applied for.

ISBN: PB: 978-1-4729-3209-9
ePDF: 978-1-4729-3211-2
ePub: 978-1-4729-3210-5

2 4 6 8 10 9 7 5 3

Designed and typeset in UK by Susan McIntyre
Printed in China

To find out more about our authors and books visit www.bloomsbury.com.
Here you will find extracts, author interviews, details of forthcoming events
and the option to sign up for our newsletters.

CONTENTS

INTRODUCTION

This book follows the classification and nomenclature usedin the comprehensive *A Guide to the Birds of Costa Rica* by F. Gary Stiles and Alexander F. Skutch published by Christopher Helm/Cornell University 1989. The measurements specified in the species descriptions are also sourced from this excellent publication.

252 species of birds are illustrated and described in this guide. This represents less than a third of the species occurring in Costa Rica but they have been selected according to what visitors are most likely to see and the species most typical of Costa Rica. This includes the only three definite species that are endemic plus a selection of regional endemics. The region referred to in this term is the ridge of highlands running through Costa Rica which continues into Panama and the Chiriqui Mountains. The antiquity and biological isolation of this region means much wildlife has developed here and nowhere else. This includes some 50 species of birds which are considered as Costa Rican specialities.

Migrants are common at certain times of year but have generally been avoided in order to allow more space for resident birds. Sea and shore birds have also been sacrificed except for a few that are commonly seen at popular locations.

Those who want to pursue their birdwatching beyond the scope of this pocket guide should refer to the Stiles and Skutch guide.

COLOURED TABS

The coloured tabs show the major family groups of birds and provide the first clues to identification. The characteristic outline for each group will lead you to the section where you should find the species you have seen.

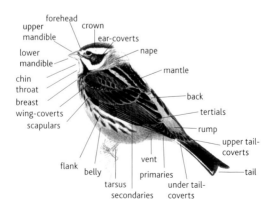

KEY TO COLOURED TABS

Tinamous

Pelicans to
frigatebirds

Herons, egrets
& storks

Ducks

Raptors

Gamebirds

Rails & allies

Waders

Gulls

Pigeons & doves

Parrots

Cuckoos & allies

Owls &
nightjars

Swifts &
hummingbirds

Trogons

Kingfishers

Motmots

Jacamars &
barbets

Toucans & allies

Woodpeckers

Woodcreepers

Ovenbirds

Antbirds

Becards, tityras
& cotingas

Manakins

American
or tyrant
flycatchers

Swallows

Jays, crows &
allies

Wrens

Thrushes &
allies

Gnatcatchers to
silky flycatchers

Vireos to
American
warblers

Orioles &
blackbirds

Tanagers

Sparrows,
finches & allies

HOW TO USE THIS BOOK

The species descriptions give each featured bird both their common and scientific name and these are followed by their length (from bill tip to the end of the tail). The text draws attention to their main identification features, including relevant behaviour and the habitats and locations where they are most likely to be found.

The classification follows that used by *A Guide to the Birds of Costa Rica* by F. Gary Stiles and Alexander F. Skutch published by Christopher Helm/Cornell University 1989. This guide is widely used so following its classification and nomenclature avoids confusion for those who wish to refer to it. Since it was published, however, some scientific and common names have been changed. These are referred to in the text.

BIRDWATCHING IN COSTA RICA

Costa Rica is part of the land bridge that joins North and South America and this partly explains its rich biodiversity. Most of the birds of the rain forests are of South American origin while those of the dry forest areas originate mainly from North America.

In spite of its small size, over 860 species of birds have been recorded in Costa Rica. To put this in perspective it is more species than occur in the USA and Canada combined. Thus it is a wonderful place for birdwatchers. The rich diversity of birds does not, however, mean that they are all easy to find or see. The forests provide a range of habitats, which house a large number of species but, equally, provide dense cover and lofty canopies to obscure them from our view. In the forests birds can be heard more often than they are seen, and when they are spotted it is often only a fleeting glimpse. Forests can be frustrating places for birdwatchers, even when a large mixed flock passes by. Then there can be an embarrassment of riches with too little time to identify all the different species flitting by. It is, though, well worth the challenge as the range of forest birds is wide and fascinating. In addition, there are many other habitats where it is easier to see birds. At some locations hummingbird feeders are provided and these are an excellent way of familiarising yourself with the species that visit them regularly.

Good birdwatching sites

Costa Rica has over 60 national parks and reserves, most of which are excellent sites for watching birds and other wildlife. To find out details of all these sites visit the Costa Rica Tourism Institute (ICT) located at the Plaza del Cultura in San José or visit their website at www. tourism-costarica.com. This website provides a wealth of information but if you need a general guide to the country once you are there *Exploring Costa Rica* published by The Tico Times is widely available, full of practical guidance and updated every year.

A comprehensive guide to good birdwatching sites is beyond the scope of this book but the following can be recommended. This does not, of course, mean that the rest are not equally rewarding, the following list is simply a taster of the many wonderful places worth visiting. To see a good range of bird species you need to visit different regions such as lowland and highland rain forests and a dry forest area. If you have time for only three regions La Selva Biological Station, Carara National Park and Cerro de la Muerte would be good choices as they provide a good range of biologically rich habitats.

The rain forests of the Caribbean slope are the most biologically rich of the country, and **La Selva Biological Station** is situated in this region. Although its main function is research, visitors are welcome. The station has some accommodation but can also be visited from the various hotels and lodges in the area.

On the Caribbean coast **Tortuguero National Park** is a good lowland rain forest site with a network of waterways and lagoons; boat trips offer opportunities for good views of monkeys, sloths, waterbirds and caimans.

Carara National Park, adjoining the south bank of the Río Grande de Tarcoles, is the northernmost outpost of the Pacific rain forest. It is an excellent park for birders where it is easy to see Scarlet Macaws and many of the Pacific forest specialities. The bridge over Río Grande de Tarcoles is a good place to view macaws as they fly in to roost in the evening and the endangered American Crocodiles dozing on sand banks in the river below.

Manuel Antonio National Park on the Pacific coast is easily reached from San José. Although it is the most 'touristy' of the national parks it has beautiful beaches, mangroves and easily observed mammals and birds.

Osa Peninsula and protected areas around the eastern shores of the Golfo Dulce, including **Golfito** and **Corcovado National Park**, is a species rich area. A good area for Squirrel Monkey, Jaguars, Baird's Tapir and Scarlet Macaws, and the only place to see the endemic Black-cheeked Tanager.

Monteverde and Santa Elena: includes Monteverde Cloud Forest Preserve, Children's Rainforest and Santa Elena Reserve. The altitudinal range is from c.1300m in Santa Elena and Monteverde on the Pacific slope, to over 1600m along the continental divide and down to c.800m on the Caribbean slope. There are good hummingbird feeders at the Hummingbird Gallery close to the entrance to the Monteverde Cloud Forest Preserve.

Braulio Carrillo National Park is adjacent to the highway and close to San José so is easily accessible and includes mid-elevation rain forest and cloud forest on the Caribbean slope. There is a good trail system at Quebrada Gonzales, the park headquarters, which provides access to rich mid-elevation forests.

Volcán Poás is the most visited national park in Costa Rica. The huge active crater is the main attraction but cloud forest rings the beautiful lake in the extinct Botos crater, providing good opportunities to see cloud forest birds and plants including many Costa Rica/Chiriqui specialities.

Cerro de la Muerte is a species-rich highland area which includes oak woodland, cloud forest and páramo and is a good place to see the Resplendent Quetzal and Costa Rica/Chiriqui specialities. I* :- ' to San José so easily accessible and also has a number of goc lodges providing accommodation.

The **Guanacaste region**, a dry forest area, includes Santa Rosa, Guanacaste and Palo Verde National Parks, Lomas de Barbudal Biological Reserve and the Nicoya beaches.

Habitats

Costa Rica has a range of mountains running more or less continuously the length of the country. West of the ridge is the Pacific slope; to the east is the Caribbean slope. The divisions are shown on the map (pages 10–11).

In spite of the small size of Costa Rica many different habitats are included. These are grouped in the text as follows:

Wet or humid tropical rain forests: Evergreen forests that are perpetually moist and damp. These conditions, combined with warmth, encourage a rich habitat of lush vegetation, tall trees and associated epiphytic growth such as mosses, bromeliads and orchids. In Costa Rica these are divided into the Caribbean and Pacific rain forests.

The **Caribbean rain forests** are archetypal tropical forests with huge trees and luxuriant growth. They are the most species rich forests in Costa Rica and the wettest part of the country.

Pacific rain forest is similar to the Caribbean forests but is isolated by the dry forests of the north and the high mountains of the Talamanca Range. This relative isolation has led to differences between the bird populations occurring on the two slopes of Costa Rica.

Cloud forest is a sub-division of the humid forest, which is restricted to higher elevations where clouds envelop the forest for much of each day. These conditions mean that the trees are not as tall as at lower altitudes but they are festooned with an even more luxuriant growth of epiphytes and lianas.

Dry forest is restricted to the northern part of the Pacific slope. Seasonal differences are more marked here than in rain forest areas. Most of the trees are deciduous and without leaves in the dry season (December to April) but respond rapidly to the arrival of the rainy season with the growth of lush green foliage.

Secondary forest is forest that has regrown after the felling of primary forest. It is less species rich than primary forest.

Inside the forest there are further divisions according to the location and height of tree growth – the understorey, mid-levels, the canopy and forest edges. The edges occur at natural gaps such as rivers and clearings as well as the boundary edge.

Non-forest habitats

Páramo in Costa Rica is found only above 3200m on the highest peaks of the Talamanca Range, above the tree line. It is a treeless area of low growth.

Coastal habitats: Rocky shorelines, beaches, marshes, mangroves, swamps (including seasonal ones), estuaries and salt flats.

Cultivated areas: Most of the forest has been cleared from lowland Costa Rica, which is now largely cattle pasture providing a savannah-type habitat, fields of sugarcane and rice and plantations of coffee, bananas and oil palm.

Residential areas: City, town and village gardens and parks.

Seasons

The wet season usually lasts from May to November but the exact start and finish is variable. In some years it can run from mid-April until mid-December or even into January. There are also variations between the Caribbean and Pacific slopes.

Although rainfall is heaviest during the rainy season, the time of day when it is likely to rain is predictable. Clouds gradually accumulate through the morning and empty their contents in the afternoon and possibly into the evening. Temperatures vary according to altitude from extremely hot on the coasts to rather chilly in the highlands. While Costa Rica is tropical it is in the northern hemisphere, so the breeding season is concentrated in April, May and June as elsewhere in that hemisphere.

FIELD TECHNIQUES FOR BIRDWATCHING

To the casual observer no equipment is necessary at all (apart from this guide book, of course) but a pair of binoculars is invaluable in aiding identification. The next most important bit of equipment is a notebook and pencil for taking field notes. When identification is in doubt there is no better substitute for working systematically through a bird's characteristics and noting them down at the time of observation, or at least as soon as possible after the bird has flown off. These notes should include a description of the location (including habitat and altitude) and the bird's behaviour and call as well as its appearance. Sketching the positions of markings such as stripes and barring can be a speedy way of noting characteristics in the field; it doesn't have to be a work of art for it to be useful when you have time to refer to a guide book.

If you are keen to add to the number of species you are going to see, the early morning is the best time for bird activity. Rainfall followed by sunshine often stimulates activity, so observing after rain can be rewarding too. It is important not to disturb wildlife while observing it, both for the sake of the wildlife and those that follow you. Always leave an area as you found it and obtain any necessary permission or permits before entering private or protected areas. Stick to designated paths, and avoid loud noises if you want to observe anything other than annoyed people.

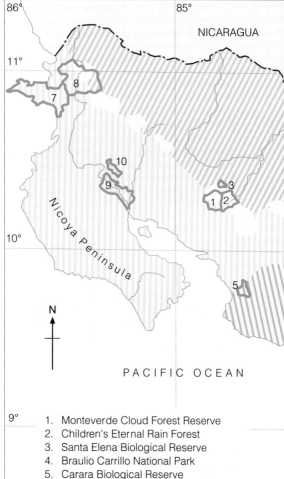

86°   85°

NICARAGUA

11°

8

7

10

9

3

1 2

10°

Nicoya Peninsula

5

N
↑

PACIFIC OCEAN

9°   1. Monteverde Cloud Forest Reserve
      2. Children's Eternal Rain Forest
      3. Santa Elena Biological Reserve
      4. Braulio Carrillo National Park
      5. Carara Biological Reserve
      6. Tortuguero National Park
      7. Santa Rosa National Park
      8. Guanacaste National Park
      9. Palo Verde National Park
      10. Lomas de Barbudal Biological Reserve
      11. Manuel Antonio National Park
      12. Volcán Poás National Park
      13. Corcovado National Park
8°   14. Golfito Reserve
      15. La Selva Biological Station

84°   83°

☐ Dry Forest
▨ Pacific Rain Forest
▨ Caribbean Rain Forest
☐ Cloud Forest
☐ Páramo
🛡 National Park & Reserve

Habitat boundaries are generalized guidelines only

CARIBBEAN SEA

6

n José

Cerro de la Muerte

PANAMA

Osa Peninsula

13

Golfo Dulce

14

0   50 miles
0   50   100 km

11

GREAT TINAMOU *Tinamus major* 43cm (17in)

A grey bird with a substantial body, short tail and thin neck topped by a small head with a slightly down-curved bill. Upperparts grey barred and mottled with black, underparts paler. Head blue-grey to black with large eyes, legs blue-grey. Both sexes are similar though the male takes charge of incubating and rearing young. They forage in the forest understorey, rarely taking flight though roost in trees at night. They have a beautiful swelling call most often heard at dusk. Commonly found in lowland rain forest of the Caribbean slope and south Pacific slope.

LITTLE TINAMOU *Crypturellus soui* 23cm (9in)

A small, plump, solitary bird with uniform brown to grey-brown colouring but always lacking the barring or mottling seen on most other tinamous. It forages secretively in dense cover but may be seen walking on trails. Although it can be difficult to see its crescendo of beautiful mellow whistles is heard frequently. It is terrestrial and feeds mostly on seeds, berries and insects. It is the most widespread of the tinamous, inhabiting overgrown scrubby areas, plantations and forest edges. It is locally common in the lowlands up to c.1500m on the Caribbean slope and on the humid parts of the Pacific slope.

BROWN PELICAN *Pelecanus occidentalis* 109cm (43in)

A large bird with an unmistakable long bill and unfeathered pouch. It has a fairly uniform dark brown plumage but with pale head and neck, yellow on the crown, short tail. Has short legs with fully webbed feet. Over six feet of wingspan give it strong flight from which it can plunge dive for prey. Flies in single file lines or Vs, alternating flaps with long glides. It is the only common pelican in Costa Rica and can often be seen following fishing boats. They can be seen on both coasts but most commonly on the Pacific side.

ANHINGA *Anhinga anhinga* 86cm (34in)

A freshwater fish eater allied to cormorants but elongated, with a long, thin bill and neck, a small head and a long fan-shaped tail. A glossy black bird with silver streaked patches on the wing coverts. The female's head and neck is a buffy brown and both sexes have a buffy brown bar at the end of the tail. The dagger shaped bill is yellow and sharply pointed, well suited to their hunting method of spearing prey underwater. When at the surface the body is often submerged leaving only the snake-like head and neck visible. This species often nests in small groups with other species of waterbirds, but it feeds alone. Occurs throughout the lowlands on both slopes at lagoons, rivers and swamps.

MAGNIFICENT FRIGATEBIRD *Fregata magnificens*
male 91cm (36in), female 111cm (44in)

This is a large, aerial seabird, mostly blackish with a deeply forked tail, long hooked bill and a 2m (6.5 foot) wingspan. Females have white on the breast and neck; immatures are similar but also have white on the head. Males have pink throat patches which are bright red during the breeding season and are inflated during display. Although associated with the sea they seldom enter the water, mostly snatching their prey from the surface and also harrying other seabirds. They occur on both coasts but are generally more abundant on the Pacific side, particularly in the Golfo de Nicoya. They breed only on offshore islands.

BARE-THROATED TIGER-HERON *Tigrisoma mexicanum*
80cm (32in)

Adult (above); juvenile (right)

This is among the larger of the herons and the combination of the grey sides to its head and its bare yellow throat distinguishes this species from other tiger-herons. The immature is buff-brown strongly barred with black. This tiger-heron has cryptic colouration, solitary habits, a loud booming call, and it frequents wooded streams and marshes. This species can be found in the lowlands of both slopes but is most easy to see in Guanacaste.

YELLOW-CROWNED NIGHT-HERON *Nyctanassa violacea*
61cm (24in)

The adults of this species are mostly grey but with a strikingly patterned black and white plumed head and yellow legs. The immatures are a dull brown speckled with white. They can be confused with the immatures of the Black-crowned Night-Heron *Nycticorax nycticorax* but are slimmer, with a heavier bill and longer legs, which are most noticeable in flight. Yellow-crowned Night-Herons tend to be most active at night, though less so than other night-herons. They are most easily seen by rivers and mangroves on both coasts.

BOAT-BILLED HERON *Cochlearius cochlearius* 51cm (20in)

This species is not dissimilar to night-herons in size and colour but its broad, shoe-like bill makes it unique. It inhabits freshwater mangrove swamps and water margins, feeding chiefly at night, a habit supported by its huge eyes. Easily seen at their communal roost sites during the day and at dusk when they leave and disperse to forage. Most likely to be seen in the lowlands on both the Caribbean and Pacific slopes.

CATTLE EGRET *Bubulcus ibis* 51cm (20in)

One of the smaller herons, mainly snowy white but with buffish patches on the head, breast and back during the breeding season. Shortish, dagger-shaped yellow bill and legs with a hint of red in the adults and a hint of black on the legs of juveniles. A common resident to be found in open fields and marsh land up to c.2000m associating with grazing animals, preying on disturbed invertebrates at their feet. They roost communally, often in huge numbers and their range is expanding as deforestation takes place.

GREEN-BACKED HERON *Butorides striatus* 43cm (17in)

This is a small heron with a maroon neck and maroon stripes on the breast. It has a black cap with an untidy crest, yellow-green facial skin, and a grey-green back. It forages in any freshwater habitat that is shallow and adjacent to cover, either alone or in pairs, and feeds on small fish, amphibians and insects. It is common and widespread throughout the country up to altitudes of c.1800m. The resident population is supplemented with the arrival of winter residents. Nowadays North and Central American birds are considered a separate species *B. virescens* from the South American version *B. striatus*.

LITTLE BLUE HERON *Egretta caerulea* 61cm (24in)

Adult (above); juvenile (right)

This is a typical slim, long-necked heron with blue-grey plumage which darkens to purple on the neck and head. Juveniles are white except for dark wing tips. They acquire adult plumage gradually so can appear patchy white and blue-grey at intermediate stages. This species feeds in both fresh and salt water habitats in the lowlands of both slopes. Common and widespread as migrants or winter residents but some non-breeding birds remain for the summer and small numbers breed intermittently.

GREAT EGRET *Casmerodius albus* 101cm (40in)

This is the largest of the white herons and has a long, slender, kinked neck and a yellow bill. It develops showy, extra long plumes on its back during the breeding season. The Snowy Egret *Egretta thula* also has entirely white plumage but is smaller and has a black bill. Great Egrets can be found foraging in both fresh and salt water marshes, estuaries, rivers and lagoons. They are common and widespread in the lowlands of both the Pacific and Caribbean coastal areas.

WOOD STORK *Mycteria americana* 102cm (40in)

This is a largely white, long-legged wading bird with a blackish, featherless head and neck. When flying, however, the black flight feathers become fully visible. They fly with the neck and legs extended. The heavy bill is slightly down curved at the tip. The superficially similar white herons and egrets do not have the black wing feathers or the bare skin of the head and neck and they often fly with the head and neck retracted. This is a very gregarious species that often hunts co-operatively in line as well as roosting communally and nesting in colonies. Most easily seen in Guanacaste and around Golfo de Nicoya.

JABIRU *Jabiru mycteria* 135cm (53in)

This huge bird has all white plumage but its naked head and neck is black with a red collar at the base. The lower mandible of the long, heavy bill is curved up, giving the impression of the bill being tilted upwards. In flight the head and neck are stretched out and, like other storks, it often soars. It forages in shallow water habitats such as marshes, swamps, ponds and lakes where it catches aquatic prey. This spectacular bird breeds only in the Tempisque Basin but can also be seen in the Caño Negro/Río Frío area.

WHITE IBIS *Eudocimus albus* 63cm (25in)

The adult of this species is largely white with just the wing tips black, which become visible in flight. It has a long, thin, down-curved bill and its red colouring extends to the bare facial skin. The legs are also red. The immatures are mostly mottled brown and lack the bright red colouring though their legs are pink. The neck is long and extended in flight. This species is gregarious and forages in the mud of both fresh and salt water. It occurs in the lowlands of both slopes but is most easily seen around the Golfo de Nicoya.

ROSEATE SPOONBILL *Ajaia ajaja* 81cm (32in)

The mostly bright pink plumage and legs and the long, spatulate bill make this species unmistakable. Adults' (shown right) heads are bare and pale green. Immatures have a feathered head, are whiter and gradually acquire the pink colouring with age. They are gregarious and feed in the shallows of both fresh and salt water by swinging the bill from side to side in order to detect their aquatic food. They can be found chiefly around the Golfo de Nicoya and less abundantly elsewhere along the Pacific coast, only rarely on the Caribbean side.

19

BLACK-BELLIED WHISTLING-DUCK *Dendrocygna autumnalis*
53cm (21in)

A duck with an upright posture and relatively long legs and neck. It has a russet neck and back, a black belly and a broad white wing bar which is particularly conspicuous in flight. The sides of the head are grey and the bill and legs are pink. Immatures are duller and lack the black belly. It is the largest whistling duck and the only one with white on the wings. It is gregarious and feeds at night mostly standing in shallow freshwater. The call is a shrill whistle usually made in flight. Resident in the lowlands of both slopes but most likely to be seen in the Tempisque Basin and Río Frío district.

TURKEY VULTURE *Cathartes aura* 76cm (30in)

The plumage appears uniform black when at rest, but the head and cere are bare and red. It has a less upright posture than Black Vulture. In flight, the grey under side of the flight feathers becomes conspicuous. When soaring the wings are held in a V-shape. It forages by flying fairly low and can locate food by smell so can access small prey below the canopy. Subordinate to Black Vulture at carcases. Seen in small numbers, except during migration when large flocks congregate. It is the most widespread of Costa Rica's vultures occurring throughout the country, though rarely above 2000m. The resident population is augmented by migrants during the winter.

BLACK VULTURE *Coragyps atratus* 64cm (25in)

An all-black vulture with an upright stance and a short tail. In flight it shows broad wings with a pale patch on the underside of the primaries. It carries its wings horizontally when soaring and has a characteristic quick wing beat when flapping. Although not actively gregarious can be seen together in thermals and at carcases, which it detects by sight alone and also homes in on groups of feeding vultures. A resident species though some of the population are thought to migrate. Occurs all over Costa Rica but is most likely to be seen around habitation and over open ground.

KING VULTURE *Sarcoramphus papa* 81cm (32in)

A large vulture with striking black and white plumage and brightly coloured skin on its bare head. The all-dark juvenile is distinctly larger than the Black and Turkey Vultures and has a heavier bill and pale eye. In flight the juvenile is more uniformly dark than the Black Vulture as it lacks the pale primaries. When soaring both adults and juveniles hold their wings in a flat position. The King Vulture uses smell to find food under the canopy but feeds mainly in open areas such as cattle country. Resident in small numbers throughout the country but good areas to find them are Guanacaste, the Osa peninsula and La Selva Biological Station.

21

OSPREY *Pandion haliaetus* 58cm (23in)

This bird of prey has long, slightly pointed, wings, which appear characteristically angled in flight with dark patches at the bend on the underside. The upperparts are dark brown contrasting with pale, almost white, underparts and a broad dark eyestripe is clear on the white of the head. Juveniles are very similar in appearance but more mottled. This species is most likely to be seen in association with large expanses of fresh or salt water where it finds its fish prey. This is mainly a migrant species found in the lowlands and foothills of both coasts but some birds remain all year round.

AMERICAN SWALLOW-TAILED KITE *Elanoides forficatus* 58cm (23in)

Its elegant outline, long, deeply forked tail and bold black and white markings make this one of the more easily identified raptors. It is most likely to be seen in flight as it hunts, feeds, and even drinks on the wing, swooping down to water like a giant swallow. It preys mostly on aerial insects but also plucks small reptiles and amphibians from trees and baby birds from nests. It favours the forested hills and mountains of humid mid-elevations on both slopes.

SEMIPLUMBEOUS HAWK *Leucopternis semiplumbea* 38cm (15in)

The plumage of this hawk is dark grey above and white below. Its tail is darker with a single white band, its cere and legs are bright orange. A compact raptor with short, broad wings equipping it well for its forest habitat where it feeds on lizards, snakes, small mammals and birds. It is a perch and pounce type predator that favours a sub-canopy position from which to hunt. The superficially similar Slaty-backed Forest-Falcon *Micrastur mirandollei* occurs in the same habitat but is larger, with longer legs, has three white bands on its tail and clear yellow cere and legs. The Semiplumbeous Hawk inhabits the forests of the lowlands and foothills of the Caribbean slope.

WHITE HAWK *Leucopternis albicollis* 56cm (22in)

A mostly white hawk with black on the wings and a black band through the tail. In flight its wings are broad and rounded and the tail fairly short. It is a forest hawk that sits in trees waiting in ambush to pounce on prey. It can also be seen soaring low over the forest canopy. It can be found in forested areas from lowland to mid-elevations on both slopes but is absent from dry forests.

COMMON BLACK-HAWK *Buteogallus anthracinus* 56cm (22in)

A mostly black raptor with a broad white band across the tail and a narrow white strip at the tip. Its legs and cere are yellow. In flight the wings are very broad and rounded and the tail is short. It tends to sit on low perches waiting to pounce on prey. Its staple diet is crabs but also takes other small prey and carrion. It is a largely coastal species occurring in watery habitats such as marshes, mangroves and rivers of both slopes. Birds inhabiting mangroves have shorter wings and are often considered a separate species, Mangrove Black-Hawk *B. subtilis*, to Common Black-Hawk.

GREY HAWK *Buteo nitidus* 41cm (16in)

The adult is a smallish grey hawk with fine barring on its undersides. The tail has a conspicuous white band, which stands out from other less distinct dark and light banding. Its relatively short, broad wings equip it well for agile flight in the woodlands in which it hunts for its prey of lizards, small mammals, large insects and birds. It sits and waits for prey as well as pursuing in flight. It is most easily found in the savannahs and forest edges of the lowlands of the northwest up to elevations of c.500m.

ROADSIDE HAWK *Buteo magnirostris* 38cm (15in)

This small hawk has a generally brownish-grey appearance but with rufous barring on its belly and rufous patches in its primaries that are conspicuous in flight. It rarely soars preferring to perch in open scrubby habitats and wait for prey to pass, mainly reptiles and large insects. It is similar in general appearance to the Broad-winged Hawk *Buteo platypterus* and Grey Hawk but the Broad-winged lacks any grey and the Grey Hawk lacks the rufous colouring. It is widespread but uncommon except in the lowlands of the north Pacific slope. Its range is spreading into deforested areas.

CRESTED CARACARA *Polyborus plancus* 61cm (24in)

This raptor has a pied look plus long, strong, yellow legs, a crested black cap, naked red skin on its face and a powerful bill. In flight there is a conspicuous white patch on the primaries. The sexes are alike and juveniles similar but browner. This species spends a lot of time on the ground though it is a strong flier. It competes for carrion with vultures and can often be seen at road kills, but it also kills its own prey in open countryside. Most easily seen in the dry northwest up to mid-elevations.

LAUGHING FALCON *Herpetotheres cachinnans* 53cm (21in)

This falcon has a white to buff body, dark brown wings and a striking black mask that extends round to the back of its head. It has a long tail which is barred black and buff. It tends to sit in wait on a high, exposed perch, ready to drop onto prey. Its main food is snakes, which it usually kills with a bite behind the head before carrying them off to a perch to eat. It is named for its cackling call and inhabits open savannah areas, secondary growth and forest edges on both slopes up to c.1500m.

BARRED FOREST-FALCON *Micrastur ruficollis*
male 33cm (13in), female 38cm (15in)

A small grey bird of prey with dark upperparts, neatly barred underparts and yellow legs. The yellow of its cere extends back to around its dark eye. It has short, rounded wings, adapted for hunting in woodland, and a long barred tail. This species favours dense cover in forests so is more likely to be heard than seen. Its call is often likened to a repetitive nasal bark and, at a distance, is not unlike that of the Highland Tinamou *Nothocercus bonapartei* but uttered more slowly, about one call every two seconds. It feeds on small reptiles, mammals and birds and also associates with army ants in order to feed on disturbed large insects. It can be found along the Caribbean and south Pacific slopes.

GREY-HEADED CHACHALACA *Ortalis cinereiceps* 51cm (20in)

A slender bird with long neck and tail and rounded wings. It is largely olive-brown with a grey head and a patch of bare red skin on the throat. It has rufous primaries which are most visible in flight and these distinguish it from the Plain Chachalaca. It moves gracefully along branches in search of fruit, berries and young leaves and is seen in loose groups of a dozen or more that stay in contact by calling to each other. It inhabits thickets and edges of secondary forests in foothills and up to c.1000m on the Caribbean slope and the south of the Pacific slope.

CRESTED GUAN *Penelope purpurascens* 86cm (34in)

The Crested Guan has olive brown plumage with a prominent crest, pale speckles on the breast and a conspicuous bare red skin flap at its throat. It is a gregarious bird with a loud honking call and is particularly noisy when going to roost at dusk. It feeds on fruit and young foliage in the canopy of forests of the lowlands and foothills of both slopes. Its numbers are being reduced by habitat loss and hunting.

BLACK GUAN *Chamaepetes unicolor* 64cm (25in)

This species has all black plumage with blue skin on its face and red legs. It is less gregarious than the Crested Guan, usually seen alone or in pairs running around in the canopy of forests at altitudes above 1000m. It suffers from hunting pressure so is common only in fairly remote or protected areas such as Monteverde Cloud Forest Preserve. It is endemic to the Costa Rica/Panama region.

SPOTTED-BELLIED BOBWHITE *Colinus leucopogon* 23cm (9in)

The spots of their name are white and more prominent on the females than the males. They are plump and both have contrasting striped markings on their head. Males have only a small crest. They are terrestrial birds that live in small groups or coveys. They forage under cover of low vegetation in savannah and scrub areas in search of seeds, berries and insects. They are common in lowlands and up to c.1500m in the dry northwest and into Valle Central through which their range reaches the Caribbean slope.

BLACK-BREASTED WOOD-QUAIL *Odontophorus leucolaemus*
23cm (9in)

This small, rotund bird is dark brown above and black below, which is flecked with white. It has a white throat, which isn't always conspicuous. It forages on the forest floor in small groups or coveys which scratch around in search of seeds, berries and some insects. The covey maintains contact by chirruping back and forth to each other. They also have a loud but beautiful call. This species inhabits humid forests of mid-elevations on both slopes but is most common on the Caribbean side. It is also known as White-throated Wood-Quail.

LIMPKIN *Aramus guarauna* 66cm (26in)

This is a large wading bird with long neck and legs and largely brown plumage. It has a long, laterally flattened, bill and a characteristic halting walk which suggests limping. Its favourite food is snails but it also takes other invertebrates and small reptiles and amphibians. It has a loud screeching call. It occurs in watery habitats such as marshes and swamps but roosts in trees. Found chiefly in the Tempisque Basin and Caño Negro region, though occasionally in other coastal areas.

SUNBITTERN *Eurypyga helias* 48cm (19in)

This wading bird is most numerous along rocky, fast-flowing rivers and forest pools where its blue-grey plumage helps it blend into the background inconspicuously , at least until it spreads its wings. The sexes are alike and their wings bear a sunburst pattern of black, chestnut and gold. This beautiful pattern is often seen when they sunbathe but the primary function of display is as a defensive threat. They are mostly terrestrial and pick their way among rocks and boulders with a hesitant but elegant gait in search of the small frogs, aquatic crustaceans and insects that they eat. Can be found in the foothills on the Caribbean slope and south Pacific slope.

NORTHERN JACANA *Jacana spinosa*
male 23cm (9in), female 25.5cm (10in)

A rail-like water bird with long legs and extra long toes that support it while walking over aquatic vegetation. Appears mostly chestnut at rest with blackish head and breast and yellow flight feathers. The large area of pale yellow on the wing shows as only a single bar when they are folded. Note the small yellow spur on the wing. A common resident in areas of undisturbed freshwater with floating vegetation, particularly in Guanacaste.

BLACK-NECKED STILT *Himantopus mexicanus* 38cm (15in)

This is an elegant bird with very long, pink legs, and long, slender neck and bill. It is black above and white below and has a white rump that is visible in flight. The long legs allow feeding in deeper water than most other waders and they extend well beyond the tail when flying. This species feeds in either salt or fresh water where it feeds on small aquatic invertebrates. It is gregarious and most likely to be seen around Guanacaste and Golfo de Nicoya.

DOUBLE-STRIPED THICK-KNEE *Burhinus bistriatus* 50cm (20in)

A dull, grey brown bird with streaks and bars that camouflage it in its favoured habitat of dry scrubby open spaces. It is most active from dusk and particularly on moonlit nights. Its night time calling is a characteristic sound of the dry forest. It looks like a wading shore bird but is restricted to the dry forest region and is a species that may have benefited from forest clearance. It is restricted to the savannas of Guanacaste.

WHIMBREL *Numenius phaeopus* 43cm (17in)

A mottled brown wader with a long, down-curved bill and conspicuous dark stripes on the crown and through the eye. It forages on the shore and occasionally on wet pastures slightly inland and feeds chiefly on marine invertebrates. Its call is a multiple whistle and it can often be seen in association with other waders. No conspicuous wing markings in flight. It is a migrant and a winter visitor seen most easily on the Pacific coast but some migrants pass on the Caribbean side and some non-breeding birds remain throughout the year.

WILLET *Catoptrophorus semipalmatus* 38cm (15in)

A large grey-brown wader, which has an upright posture and a heavy straight bill. It has a striking black and white wing pattern visible only in flight. The photograph shows its summer plumage, in winter it lacks the dark spotting and barring. It forages in coastal areas and feeds on marine molluscs, crustaceans and small fish. It often perches on poles and joins large, mixed flocks of wading birds when not foraging. It is a migrant and winter resident most commonly on the Pacific coast, and an occasional non-breeding resident. Less common on the Caribbean coast.

SPOTTED SANDPIPER *Actitis macularia* 19cm (7.5in)

Breeding (left); non-breeding (right)

This is a rather nondescript wader in winter plumage when it has brown upper parts and white below, yellow legs and white above the eye with a dark stripe through it. In summer the eye markings are more defined with dark barring on the back and bold spotting on the underparts. Its most characteristic feature is its forward tilted gait and continuous wagging of the rump and tail. It also has a distinctive, stiff-winged flight and a frequently used peet-weet call. A migrant visitor that is widespread and occurs in all waterside habitats up to c.1800m. Moults into breeding plumage before migrating north in April/May.

RUDDY TURNSTONE *Arenaria interpres* 22cm (8.75in)

Breeding (left); non-breeding (right)

The breeding plumage of this wader is rufous and black on the back with a black chest but otherwise white underparts. The head has bold black markings and a distinctive pattern shows on the wings in flight. The bill looks slightly upturned at the tip. The bird on the left is still in winter plumage which has less contrasting colours. They forage mainly in inter-tidal zones, flicking aside pebbles and seaweed in search of invertebrates. Roosts in flocks. A migrant and winter visitor to both coasts and, rarely, a non-breeding summer visitor.

LAUGHING GULL *Larus atricilla* 40cm (16in)

Adult (left); juvenile (right)

This gull has a black head and bill, white eye-ring, white neck and underparts and dark grey on the back during the breeding season (left) and the wings are tipped with black. The immature (right) lacks the well defined black head and has some dark mottling. It resembles the adult in non-breeding plumage. This species takes its name from its cackling call which vaguely resembles laughter. It feeds mostly in coastal areas but also ventures inland along the bigger rivers. A migrant and winter resident, and occasionally non-breeding summer resident, mostly on the Pacific coast and particularly at Golfo de Nicoya.

BAND-TAILED PIGEON *Columba fasciata* 35cm (14in)

This is the largest of the pigeons to be found in Costa Rica. It is largely purplish-grey with a conspicuous white collar edged with iridescent green. Bill and legs are yellow and the long rounded tail has a single broad dark band. Other large pigeons are smaller, ruddier and lack the yellow bill and legs and white collar. This species is a strong, direct flier, which is often seen flying high over forest canopy. It gathers in flocks and feeds on the fruits and berries that occur in highland forests throughout the country.

PALE-VENTED PIGEON *Columba cayennensis* 30cm (12in)

A pigeon which is purple-brown on its back, with a grey head and iridescent green on the nape. Its underparts are largely pale pinkish-brown but its white lower belly and under tail area are diagnostic. It feeds on fruits in lightly wooded areas and forest clearings and borders. It inhabits the humid lowlands of the Caribbean and southern Pacific slopes up to c.600m, particularly favouring coastal areas. Short-billed Pigeon (see below) is similar but smaller, lacks the white on the underparts and prefers a forest habitat.

SHORT-BILLED PIGEON *Columba nigrirostris* 26.5cm (10.5in)

A fairly uniformly coloured pigeon of purple-brown, darkest on the wings and palest on the belly. It has a short black bill and pink-red eye-rings and legs. It favours the forest canopy but also forages at lower levels for fruits, berries and some insects. It inhabits the humid lowlands up to c.1100m on the Caribbean slope and the south Pacific slope. Very similar to Ruddy Pigeon *C. subvinacea* which is more rufous and more uniformly coloured and replaces Short-billed in highland forests. Where their ranges overlap they are best told apart by their calls.

WHITE-WINGED DOVE *Zenaida asiatica* 27cm (10.75in)

A buffy-brown pigeon with a pink wash on the breast and a white wing bar, which is conspicuous both at rest and in flight. The outer tail feathers are white tipped and there is a black streak below the eye. It perches in trees but forages on the ground in dry areas of savannah or open woodland. A social bird that roosts in flocks. The resident population is concentrated in the dry northwest lowlands, occasionally as far east as San José. Their numbers are supplemented by the arrival of migrant winter residents.

COMMON GROUND-DOVE *Columbina passerina* 16cm (6.25in)

A tiny, pinkish-grey dove with darker markings giving it a scaly appearance around its head and breast. In flight its rufous primaries are conspicuous. The sexes are similar but the female is generally duller. They are usually seen in pairs but also flocks in winter and their call is a soft coo. They forage on the ground for seeds and occasional insects and are often seen collecting grit from roads. They prefer open and shrubby areas particularly in dry regions. Can be found commonly in the north Pacific lowlands.

RUDDY GROUND-DOVE *Columbina talpacoti* 16.5cm (6.5in)

Male (left); female (right)

A reddish-brown pigeon, paler underneath and darkest on the wings, which are flecked with black. The head is pale grey. The female has duller colouring and a buff head only tinged with grey. They frequent open areas of agricultural and residential lowlands, and forage on the ground in pairs or small groups. They are often seen on roads and tracks where they gather grit. They feed on seeds and berries and roost together in trees or shrubs. It is common in deforested parts of the Caribbean lowlands and south Pacific slope up to altitudes of c.1200m.

INCA DOVE *Columbina inca* 20cm (8in)

A small, dove of brownish-grey with a scaled pattern. It has a long tail with white outer stripes and in flight its chestnut primary feathers are revealed. It is largely terrestrial. Males call from perches with their two note coos. This dove is social and roosts communally as well as foraging in pairs or small groups. It is abundant and can be found commonly in open or sparsely wooded areas in the north western lowlands and is expanding its range southward. Some authorities place this species in the genus *Scardafella*.

WHITE-TIPPED DOVE *Leptotila verreauxi* 26cm (10.25in)

This is a solitary dove that has brown back and wings and pinkish-grey underparts. It has a narrow blue ring around the eye which can be seen at close quarters. Its most conspicuous feature is the broad white tips to its outer tail feathers, which are most easily seen in flight. It is more evenly coloured than Grey-chested Dove and has more white on the tail. It is largely terrestrial and inhabits fairly open areas such as deciduous woodland, plantations and gardens, where it forages on the ground but flies to cover when disturbed. It is common throughout lowlands the length of the Pacific slope and may be extending its range. Also known as White-fronted Dove.

GREY-CHESTED DOVE *Leptotila cassinii* 24cm (9.5in)

Caribbean form (above); Pacific form (right)

This is a largely grey dove with buffish-grey on the wings and red skin around the eye. It has white tips to its outer tail feathers but they are smaller than on White-tipped Dove (see above). The example on the left is the Caribbean form; the Pacific form on the right shows its rufous nape and crown. This species forages in the more open areas of forest understorey extending also into gardens and plantations. It forages alone or in pairs but also associates with White-tipped Dove. It occurs on the Caribbean and southern Pacific slopes, commonly up to mid-elevations.

SCARLET MACAW *Ara macao* 84cm (33in)

An unmistakable bird with spectacularly colourful plumage, a long tail and noisy habits. It occurs in flocks and used to be common throughout the lowlands of Costa Rica. Unfortunately their numbers have declined and they are now seen easily only on the Osa Peninsula and around Carara National Park.

ORANGE-FRONTED PARAKEET *Aratinga canicularis* 22.5cm (9in)

This largely green parakeet has an orange forehead, a small area of blue on its crown and bare yellow skin around the eyes. It has a long pointed tail and blue primaries. It is a highly social species traveling and feeding in noisy flocks and also roosting communally. They are fast fliers and feed on the seeds, fruit and flowers in areas of sparse woodland, secondary growth and forest edges. They can be seen on the north Pacific slope up to mid-elevations. This species is exploited for the caged bird trade and has seen a decrease in population numbers. The related Crimson-fronted Parakeet *A. finschi* is the largest of the parakeets and is common on the Caribbean slope and in the Valle Central including in San José.

ORANGE-CHINNED PARAKEET *Brotogeris jugularis* 18cm (7in)

This small green parakeet has an orange spot on its chin, brown shoulders, and a patch of yellow on the under wing which is visible in flight. It has a fairly short, pointed tail. It is tinged with blue on the head, rump, primaries and tail. The shape and relative length of the tail, combined with its markings help to distinguish it from other green parakeets. It occurs in noisy flocks in open areas and at forest edges though the flocks tend to break up during the breeding season. It is most common in the north Pacific lowlands but is expanding its range following deforestation.

WHITE-FRONTED PARROT *Amazona albifrons* 25cm (10in)

A medium-sized, green parrot with a short tail and a conspicuous white patch on its forehead and blue on its crown. Its face has a red mask and the male also has red on the wings. This is a gregarious species that may travel in flocks of up to 50 birds on the north Pacific slope. Amazona parrots have fluttering flight with shallow wing beats. The only other green parrot with white on its face is the White-crowned Parrot *Pionus senilis*, which flies with deep wing beats and occurs only on the Caribbean side, so their ranges do not overlap.

RED-LORED PARROT *Amazona autumnalis* 34cm (13.5in)

This Amazona parrot is mostly green, but has red above the bill, yellowish-green cheeks and a lavender tinge to the head. A red patch on the wings (the speculum) is visible in flight but appears as only a small bar when at rest. The red on the face is characteristic of this species but it can be difficult to separate the *Amazona* parrots, especially in flight, though their different calls are helpful. It is a parrot of the forest edges and, like most of this group, is gregarious and noisy, with a rather metallic call. It occurs in the lowlands and foothills of the Caribbean slope and the south of the Pacific side.

MEALY PARROT *Amazona farinosa* 38cm (15in)

One of the larger green parrots with a relatively short blunt tail. It lacks the bright splashes of colour on the head of other *Amazona* parrots but it is tinged with blue and the eye is circled with white bare skin. The red and blue on the wings are not very visible except when in flight. It is gregarious and very noisy when flying but less so when feeding. It favours humid forested areas of the lowlands of the Caribbean and south Pacific slopes but its range is being reduced by deforestation and numbers by the cage-bird trade.

SQUIRREL CUCKOO *Piaya cayana* 46cm (18in)

This species is named for its habit of running along branches like a squirrel. Its appearance is dominated by its long tail, which is strongly patterned on the underside with bold white ends to the feathers. It is particularly fond of caterpillars, even those with irritating hairs. It lives at forest edges including secondary growth and occurs throughout Costa Rica, though is rare at high altitudes.

GROOVE-BILLED ANI *Crotophaga sulcirostris* 30cm (12in)

This species is an all-black member of the cuckoo family with a heavy, grooved bill that is compressed laterally and gives the bird a characteristic outline. It has a long tail, which appears loosely attached and floppy. It is very social, feeding and roosting in loose groups and even nesting co-operatively with several females laying in the same nest. Feeds mainly on invertebrates, often in association with cattle preying on the insects they disturb. It is very similar to the Smooth-billed Ani but has a less humped bill, and their ranges overlap only slightly. It can be seen throughout the country up to c.2300m altitude, but is largely displaced by the Smooth-billed in the south Pacific regions.

SMOOTH-BILLED ANI *Crotophaga ani* 35cm (14in)

This member of the cuckoo family is very similar to the Grooved-billed Ani but is a little larger. It is all black, with a long tail and is rather disheveled looking. It has a heavy, laterally flattened bill, and the high crown of the upper mandible gives a humped, diagnostic outline. It is highly gregarious, including nesting co-operatively, and it feeds mainly on insects often in association with livestock. It can often be seen sunbathing, as in the photograph. It prefers open habitats and occurs commonly in the south Pacific regions up to altitudes of c.1200m, where it has largely displaced the Groove-billed Ani. Its range is currently spreading north.

LESSER GROUND-CUCKOO *Morococcyx erythropygius* 25cm (10in)

This bird's most striking feature is its facial pattern, which has yellow and blue bare skin outlined in black. There is a narrow white stripe along the brow and the bill is substantial and slightly down-curved. It is rufous below and grey-brown with a glossy sheen above. It forages mostly on the ground in search of invertebrates and prefers fairly open habitats such as savannah and woodland borders. It occurs in the north of the Pacific slope up to altitudes of c.1200m.

43

PACIFIC SCREECH-OWL *Otus cooperi* 23cm (9in)

This is a grey-brown owl with darker streaking, the facial disc outlined in brown and with obvious ear-like tufts. The tufts or horns are missing from juveniles. Paler than Tropical Screech-Owl *Otus choliba* and the facial disc is less clearly defined. Inhabits open woodland and savannah where it hunts at night starting soon after dusk. Its call is a long series of nasal hoots. Its hunting strategy is to sit on low perches and pounce or sally for large invertebrates. Common in the northwest on the Pacific slope in the lowlands and up to c.1000m.

VERMICULATED SCREECH-OWL *Otus guatemalae* 20cm (8in)

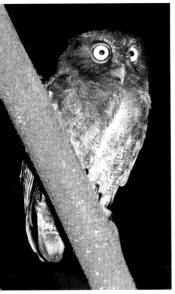

Four species of screech-owl occur in Costa Rica and all are rather similar. The Vermiculated has, however, a softly dappled plumage that is less strongly marked with bars and streaks than its cousins. This small owl also has a less well marked facial disc than other screech-owls and fairly inconspicuous ear-tufts. Its soft trilling call belies its name. It is common and widespread in primary forest and old secondary growth in the Caribbean lowlands and in the south of the Pacific slope.

CRESTED OWL *Lophostrix cristata* 40cm (16in)

One of the larger owls of Costa Rica with long ear-tufts that are accentuated by white feathers that form a distinctive V, particularly when the tufts are raised in alarm. The wings also bear conspicuous pale spots. Its call is a gruff, growling noise that is characteristic at night in the lowland forests it favours. It prefers primary and old secondary forests and is widespread in these habitats throughout the lowlands and foothills on both slopes.

SPECTACLED OWL *Pulsatrix perspicillata* 48cm (19in)

This owl's large size and heavily spectacled appearance make it very distinctive and not easily confused with other species. It has mainly rich, dark brown plumage but with a pale breast and no ear-tufts. It lives in dense forest but prefers to hunt in the more open clearings. The main call sounds like sheet metal being wobbled and pairs can often be heard calling back and forth to each other. It is widespread, but not numerous, throughout Costa Rica up to 1500m.

FERRUGINOUS PYGMY-OWL *Glaucidium brasilianum*
15cm (6in)

A diminutive, earless owl with a relatively long tail. Often active during the day as well as night. Brown above, white with heavy brown streaking below. It has two dark spots outlined in white on its nape that give the impression of false eyes. It has two colour forms, one brown and the other more rufous. It hunts in wooded areas including plantations and suburbia. Its prey is mostly invertebrates and some lizards. This species inhabits the lowlands of the north Pacific slope. It is very similar to the Least Pygmy-Owl *Glaucidium minutissimum* of the Caribbean slopes but their ranges do not overlap. Also difficult to differentiate from the slightly larger Andean Pygmy-Owl *Glaucidium jardinii*, which has more distinct spotting on head and breast.

BLACK-AND-WHITE OWL *Ciccaba nigrolineata* 38cm (15in)

A dark, brownish-black owl which has fine black and white barring on its underparts and a yellow beak. Difficult to see because of its nocturnal habits except at diurnal roosts e.g. at trees in the town square of Orotina, a good place to see this species. It favours forests and woodlands but often hunts on the edges in search of its prey of large insects and small mammals. Calls include a series of deep hoots and a nasal yowl. Not a numerous species but occurs in the lowlands and foothills on the Caribbean slope and the more northerly Pacific slope.

LESSER NIGHTHAWK *Chordeiles acutipennis* 22cm (8.75in)

This bird is barred and streaked in browns and greys that make it very difficult to distinguish in its daytime resting position. In flight the dark tips of its wings become apparent and the white band on the primaries (buff on females) is conspicuous. The throat has a white (male) or buff (female, as shown) band. The bill appears small but it has a huge gape for catching insects in flight. It hawks and sallies for insects from late afternoon through the night until early morning in open, scrubby areas. The resident population favours lowland coastal areas on the Pacific slope but migrants and winter visitors are also seen on the Caribbean slope.

COMMON PAURAQUE *Nyctidromus albicollis* 28cm (11in)

This species has soft loose plumage that is brown and cryptically-streaked and mottled so it blends imperceptibly with its surroundings. It relies on its camouflage, even when predators are very close, and moves only at the last possible moment, particularly when nesting. It is most likely to be seen at night, hawking for insects when its long wings and very long tail are apparent. Also commonly seen in headlights on dirt roads at night when its eyes give a ruby-red eye-shine. Common and widespread.

WHITE-COLLARED SWIFT *Streptoprocne zonaris* 22cm (8.75in)

The largest of the swifts occurring in Costa Rica and entirely dull black except for the conspicuous white collar. The tail is slightly notched and is fanned when the bird is soaring. The beak appears insignificant but the gape is very large. They are social and often occur in large flocks, and nest in caves. Like all swifts they are exceptional fliers and use this ability to forage countrywide for their insect food. Although they can be seen throughout the country they favour feeding over humid low and mid altitudes while tending to roost and nest at higher elevations.

LONG-TAILED HERMIT *Phaethornis superciliosus* 15cm (6in)

This hermit is one of the less brightly coloured hummingbirds which has a long down-curved bill, conspicuous facial stripes and a long tail. It feeds by visiting as many flowers as possible on a long route through the forest; by the time it goes round the route again the flowers have replenished their nectar supply. It can be distinguished from other hermits by the combination of its brownish plumage and long tail. It is common in lowland rain forests all along the Caribbean slope and the southern half of the Pacific side.

GREEN HERMIT *Phaethornis guy* 15cm (6in)

They have glossy green plumage tinged with blue and long down-curved bills. The female has a longer tail than the male (similar to the Long-tailed Hermit) and also has clear facial stripes that are very pale or missing on the male. Like other hermits this species has a regular foraging route. As with Long-tailed Hermit, males gather in loose leks during the breeding season but otherwise this species tends to be solitary. Its rich iridescent green colouring differentiates it from the mostly brown Long-tailed Hermit. It is chiefly found in the wet forests of mid to high elevations on both slopes.

VIOLET SABREWING *Campylopterus hemileucurus* 15cm (6in)

Male (above); female (right)

A large, robust hummingbird the male of which is deep violet. Both sexes have prominent white patches on either side of the end of the tail and a down-curved bill. The female is of equal size but is less brightly coloured, her violet feathers being confined to her gorget. Violet Sabrewings are mainly trapliners but their size means they can also steal from other birds' territories in the forest understorey. Common in highlands, particularly in cloud forest, and on both slopes above c.1000m but often lower outside the breeding season. They visit hummingbird feeders at Monteverde and in the Sarapiquí Valley.

BROWN VIOLETEAR *Colibri delphinae* 11.5cm (4.5in)

A generally brown hummingbird with a straight, relatively short, bill. The rump is cinnamon, the gorget a brilliant green, the face mask violet and the tail has a dark band above cinnamon trailing edge. It favours the canopy of forest habitats but descends at edges and clearings. Breeds mainly at mid-elevations on the Caribbean slope but is easiest to see after the breeding season when it disperses to both lower and higher elevations. From late April to June, or later, it is a regular visitor to hummingbird feeders at La Paz Waterfall Garden and Mirador Cinchona in the Sarapiquí Valley, and Monteverde.

GREEN VIOLETEAR *Colibri thalassinus* 10.5cm (4in)

Unusually in hummingbirds, the male and female are alike in this species. They are predominantly green and have distinctive violet ear patches and a dark band across the tail. Their bills are very slightly down-curved. Their ear patches mean they are unlikely to be confused with other species. Males can often be heard singing repetitively from high in a tree. They are common in forests of the highlands preferring more open habitats including deforested areas. They commonly come to bird feeders.

GREEN-BREASTED MANGO *Anthracothorax prevostii*
12cm (4.75in)

Male (above); immature (right)

Both sexes have green upperparts and a bill that is slightly down-curved. The male is also green below but with a blackish-violet patch extending from the throat to the belly, and a purple tail. The female resembles the immature but lacks rufous edging to white underparts. Occasionally some females resemble the males. A lowland species that prefers savanna and open woodland, its range is extending into deforested areas. It inhabits the north of both the Caribbean and Pacific slopes, often common locally.

VIOLET-HEADED HUMMINGBIRD *Klais guimeti* 7.5cm (3in)

The Violet-headed Hummingbird is tiny, weighing less than 3g. The male is distinctive with a brilliant violet-blue forehead, crown and throat. The female has a greener blue on the crown only. The small but conspicuous squarish white spot behind the eye is the most useful identification aid for both sexes. This species frequents the canopy, second growth, clearings, and also gardens close to forest. It is common below c.1000m on the Caribbean and south Pacific slopes but seldom ventures away from the foothills.

CROWNED WOODNYMPH *Thalurania colombica*
male 10cm (4in), female 9cm (3.5in)

The male's glittering plumage makes him one of the most beautiful hummingbirds with violet-blue and green and a deeply forked, blue-black tail. The female is mostly green with a well defined pale grey throat and chest, lacking any violet-blue and the tail is only slightly forked with white tips to the outer points. During the breeding season the male feeds in the canopy while the female concentrates mainly on the forest understorey. A common resident of wet forests of the Caribbean and south Pacific slopes.

FIERY-THROATED HUMMINGBIRD *Panterpe insignis*
11cm (4.25in)

Unmistakable if you catch the blue crown and breast and glittering red and orange gorget but the iridescence may appear simply dark unless viewed from head-on and above. Otherwise they are glossy dark green with a blue-black tail and a white spot behind the eye. Both sexes look the same and defend territories aggressively. This species is common in cloud forest areas at high elevations, visits feeders and is easily seen on Poás and Irazú Volcanoes and the Cerro de la Muerte. There is some altitudinal migration after breeding.

MANGROVE HUMMINGBIRD *Amazilia boucardi* 9.5cm (3.75in)

Male (above); female (right)

This species has a conspicuous white belly, which on the female extends up to the throat. The male's throat and chest is a bright blue-green while the female has a paler green flanking the white of her throat and chest. Other hummingbirds are similar but this species' range is restricted to mangroves and adjacent areas where it is unlikely to be confused with other white bellied hummingbirds. Its principal food source is the nectar of Pacific Mangrove flowers though it visits other flowers as well. Found in the mangroves of the Pacific coast between Golfo de Nicoya and Golfo Dulce and endemic to Costa Rica.

CINNAMON HUMMINGBIRD *Amazilia rutila* 9.5cm (3.75in)

This hummingbird has characteristic cinnamon underparts, paler at the throat and darkening to rufous on the tail, upperparts bronzy-green. The sexes are similar but the male (shown) has a mostly red bill while the female's is mainly black. They are aggressive territorialists. This species favours deciduous woodland, in secondary growth and open scrubby areas. It is a resident of the Pacific slope south to Río Tarcoles, mainly to 500m.

RUFOUS-TAILED HUMMINGBIRD *Amazilia tzacatl* 10cm (4in)

As its name suggests, this species has a rufous tail. The rest of the plumage is mainly bronzy-green. The sexes are similar but the female's throat and chest are more mottled. It is an active and aggressive species that is commonly seen in open scrub and areas of habitation including gardens in San José. It is widespread and common on both the Caribbean and Pacific slopes in lowlands and foothills.

BLACK-BELLIED HUMMINGBIRD *Eupherusa nigriventris* 8cm (3.25in)

The male has a black face and underparts, most of the tail white but darker down the centre, with a rufous patch on the wing. The female differs by having grey underparts. She is very similar to the female Striped-tailed Hummingbird *Eupherusa eximia* but has more white on the tail and the rufous on the wing is inconspicuous. They live in wet forests, the male favouring the canopy while the female often forages at lower levels, at edges and gaps. They inhabit the Caribbean slope at mid-elevations, between c.900–2000m during breeding season but may descend lower at other times. They visit feeders in Sarapiquí Valley. A regional endemic.

COPPERY-HEADED EMERALD *Elvira cupreiceps* 7.5cm (3in)

Male (above); female (right)

One of the smaller hummingbirds, the male has copper on his crown, rump and the centre of the tail. The outer tail feathers are conspicuously white. The female has white underparts and a rather smudged black band just above the end of the tail. Both have slightly down-curved bills. They forage at most levels and out to edges and clearings. They are endemic to Costa Rica and inhabit chiefly the Caribbean slope between altitudes c.700–1500m but may descend lower outside the breeding season. They reach the Pacific slope via passes in the north only.

PURPLE-THROATED MOUNTAIN-GEM *Lampornis calolaema* 10.5cm (4in)

Female (above); Male (right)

Only the male has a purple throat. He has a blackish tail and is otherwise mainly green. Both the male and female have a white stripe running from the back of the eye. The female has rufous underparts and a white tip to her dull black tail. They favour the canopy of forested hills but will forage down to lower levels. Males are fiercely territorial at a good food source while females are trapliners. They prefer forests of mid-elevation chiefly on the Caribbean slope. The classification of this species is disputed, some authorities regard it and similar species as Variable Mountain-gem *L. castaneoventris*.

GREY-TAILED MOUNTAIN-GEM *Lampornis cinereicauda*
10.5cm (4in)

Both sexes of this species are similar to those of the Purple-throated Mountain-gem but the male has a white gorget and the female a duller tail. Their habits are also similar but their ranges only slightly overlap. This species mostly replaces Purple-throated in Cordillera de Talamanca where it inhabits the oak forests south to Panama. Comes readily to feeders. A virtual endemic but its range probably extends into Panama and its classification as a separate species is disputed.

GREEN-CROWNED BRILLIANT *Heliodoxa jacula*
male 13cm (5in), female 12cm (4.75in)

Male (above); female (right)

This is one of the larger hummingbirds, mostly green and with a straight bill. The male has a small purple patch on its throat and the female has pale underparts spotted heavily with green. The male has a long, strongly forked tail, the female's is shorter with white tips. They both have a small white patch behind the eye and the female has a white stripe below her eye. They frequent humid highland forests and prefer to perch rather than hover at flowers when feeding. They can be found at elevations from c.700–c.2000m on both slopes but chiefly the Caribbean side. An area endemic.

MAGNIFICENT HUMMINGBIRD *Eugenes fulgens* 13cm (5in)

Male (above); female (right)

One of the larger hummingbirds, which has a relatively long, straight bill. The male has a purple forehead and crown, brilliant green throat and white spot behind the eye. The green of his breast and back is tinged with bronze. The female has buffy grey underparts, a white tip to the tail and a white stripe at the back of the eye. This is a highland species frequenting oak forests of Cordilleras Central and de Talamanca from c.2000m to the tree line and can be seen at feeders at Cerro de la Muerte. Sometimes regarded as a different species from the North American Magnificent Hummingbird.

MAGENTA-THROATED WOODSTAR *Calliphlox bryantae*
male 9cm (3.5in), female 7.5cm (3in)

This is one of the smaller hummingbirds, the male of which has a brilliant magenta gorget fringed along its lower edge with white. He has buffy patches on the sides of the rump and a forked tail. The female also has pale patches at the side of the rump but has rufous on her underparts, the white collar on her throat is less distinct and the tail shorter. They prefer relatively open parts of forests and are sometimes territorial at suitable flowers. They occur along the Pacific slope, occasionally reaching the Caribbean side at passes in the north. A local species but easily seen from October to April at Monteverde. An area endemic.

SCINTILLANT HUMMINGBIRD *Selasphorus scintilla*
6.5cm (2.5in)

A tiny bird, the male of which has a flamboyant orange-red gorget, extended at the sides and fringed with white on its lower edge. His tail is rufous with black stripes and his underparts are largely rufous with green markings. The female is more rufous below and the throat buff with dark markings. The rufous of her tail is broken by a black band towards the end. They prefer relatively open habitats such as forest edges, plantations and scrub where they visit flowers with easily accessible nectar and where they often compete with insects. Resident at altitudes of c.900–2100m mainly on the Pacific slope. An area endemic.

VOLCANO HUMMINGBIRD *Selasphorus flammula* 7.5cm (3in)

Male (above); female (right)

The male of this species is green above, white below with green on the flanks and variable throat colour and tail markings depending on location. His gorget can be greyish purple (Talamanca), purple (Irazú-Turrialba) or red (Poas-Barva) and the tail black with varying amounts of rufous stripes and green central feathers. The female has a white throat with dark flecking and a white tip to the tail. Its small size means it feeds largely at insect pollinated flowers. A bird of the open highlands above c.1800m including páramo and into elfin forest. An altitudinal migrant that descends to lower altitudes outside the breeding season. An area endemic.

RESPLENDENT QUETZAL *Pharomachrus mocinno*
36cm (14in) plus 64cm (25in) for male's tail streamers

The male is the most ornate and spectacular of the trogons, resplendent in his bright green plumage with a brilliant red breast, a small crest, white tail feathers and elongated upper tail coverts. The female is more like other trogons, with a grey-brown breast, less iridescence and with a barred tail which lacks the elongated streamers. It eats fruit, particularly wild avocados, which they pluck in flight. During the breeding season the males attract attention by their loud calls and spectacular display flight high above the canopy, cackling like a demented chicken. Breed in cloud forests but move to lower altitudes for part of the year. Most easily seen at Cerro de la Muerte, Poás and Monteverde.

Female (above); male (right)

SLATY-TAILED TROGON *Trogon massena* 30cm (12in)

This species has the typical upright stance of the trogons, which shows off its bright red belly and uniform dark grey tail. The male has a rich green on the back and an orange red bill. The female is greyer and only the lower mandible of the bill is reddish. This species favours the canopy and higher levels of wet lowland forests but also forages in clearings. It inhabits the humid areas of the foothills of the Caribbean slope and the southern Pacific slope. Superficially similar to Lattice-tailed Trogon *Trogon clathratus* but which has a yellow bill and a barred tail.

BAIRD'S TROGON *Trogon bairdii* 28cm (11in)

This trogon's blue eye-ring is diagnostic within the red-bellied trogons and the belly colour is a distinctive deep orangey-red. The female is similar to the female Slaty-tailed Trogon (see p59) but has less red and the bill is bluish-grey like the eye-ring. This species inhabits the upper levels of the rain forest where it feeds on fruits, insects, amphibians and small reptiles plucked from trees in flight then taken to a perch for eating. It can be found in the lowlands and foothills of the south Pacific slope and is an area endemic with its range extending from Costa Rica into southwest Panama.

BLACK-HEADED TROGON *Trogon melanocephalus* 27cm (10.5in)

This is one of the yellow bellied trogons and the male is shown in the illustration. The male's back is iridescent green which becomes blue at the rump. The upper tail is bluish-green. The female is largely slaty grey above and on her head and breast. The white tips to the tail feathers are narrower on the female giving a more barred pattern. The species inhabits deciduous woodland and tall secondary forest, where it finds the fruit and insects it eats. It can be found in most of the lowlands and hills of the Pacific slope but chiefly in the more northern regions.

ORANGE-BELLIED TROGON *Trogon aurantiiventris* 25cm (10in)

Female (above); male (right)

The colourful orange to orangey-red belly of this species is separated from the darker upperparts by a conspicuous white band. The sexes differ as shown. This species is very similar to Collared Trogon *Trogon collaris*, the only difference being that Collared has a redder belly; even their calls are the same. Some authorities consider them as different colour phases of the same species. They are fruit-eaters in the humid forests of mid to upper elevations of the central highlands, becoming scarcer in the more southern regions.

BLACK-THROATED TROGON *Trogon rufus* 23cm (9in)

A yellow-bellied trogon; the male has metallic green breast and upper parts and a black face and throat, a pale blue eye-ring and a greenish- yellow bill. The female has a duller yellow belly and a buff breast, head and back. She also has a blue eye-ring but her upper mandible is mostly black. The female is the only trogon to combine brown and yellow plumage. They have the typical trogon feeding habit of taking insects and fruit in flight and frequent the low and middle levels of humid forests. They inhabit the humid lowlands of the Caribbean and south Pacific slopes.

VIOLACEOUS TROGON *Trogon violaceus* 23cm (9in)

One of the smaller trogons and with a yellow belly. The male has a blue head and breast, a yellow eye-ring and black and white barring on the under tail feathers. The female has dark grey head and back and her uneven eye-ring is greyish-white. They have the typical trogon foraging habits of perching, sallying and plucking fruits and insects while hovering. They prefer relatively open habitats like forest edges and occur in both dry and humid areas but are less numerous in dry regions. They inhabit both slopes from lowlands up to c.1000m.

RINGED KINGFISHER *Ceryle torquata* 41cm (16in)

This is Costa Rica's largest kingfisher. It is rufous below and slate grey above and with a heavy dagger shaped bill. The female, as shown in the illustration, has slate grey on the breast separated from the rufous by a narrow white band. This grey-blue breast is absent in the male but they are otherwise similar. They have a bushy crest that can be more apparent than in the image. It hunts in both fresh and salt water frequenting rivers, lakes and estuaries and plunges from higher perches than most kingfishers. It can be seen in the lowlands along both slopes, usually in association with water.

AMAZON KINGFISHER *Chloroceryle amazona* 29cm (11.5in)

This kingfisher is dark metallic green above with a white collar but only light spotting of white on wings and tail. They have a heavy, dark bill and a crest. The undersides are white with a rufous band on the breast of the male, replaced with green on the sides of the breast of the female (shown), with some green spotting in the middle forming a broken band. They favour wide expanses of water such as broad rivers, estuaries and mangrove channels where they dive for fish. They can be found at water habitats on both coasts up to altitudes of c.900m.

GREEN KINGFISHER *Chloroceryle americana* 18cm (7in)

Male (above); female (right)

This is one of the smaller kingfishers and is green above and white below with green spotting down its sides. The male has a rufous breast band while the female has two narrower green breast bands. Both have white spots on the wings and outer tail feathers which are conspicuous in flight. Amazon Kingfisher *Chloroceryle amazona* is similar in appearance but is much larger and lacks the conspicuous white spotting on wings and tail. Green Kingfishers hunt by small streams and pools that occur in lowlands and mid-elevations of both slopes.

BROAD-BILLED MOTMOT *Electron platyrhynchum* 30.5cm (12in)

Has the typical upright stance of the motmots, slightly down-curved bill and long tail. It has a dark face mask, rufous head and chest, a green back and belly and a dark spot in the middle of its chest. The central tail feathers are likely to have racquet tips where weak barbs have broken off the shaft. These, however, are sometimes missing. It feeds mainly on invertebrates, small frogs and lizards but also some fruit. It often attracts attention with its harsh croaking call. This species inhabits the lower humid forests of the Caribbean slope.

TURQUOISE-BROWED MOTMOT *Eumomota superciliosa* 34cm (13.5in)

A colourful bird with a conspicuous pale turquoise stripe above the eye and longer shafts to the tail racquets than other motmots. It has a mainly rufous body with a black mask and throat and turquoise-green wings. As with other motmots, this species sits for long periods with an upright stance, and occasionally sallies forth for passing insects or small reptiles. It has a rough croaking call. It inhabits the open scrubby areas and deciduous woodlands of the north Pacific slope.

RUFOUS MOTMOT *Baryphthengus martii* 46cm (18in)

This is the largest Costa Rican motmot. Its head, neck and breast are rufous and back green with blue on the wings that is most visible in flight. It has a striking black mask and a small black chest spot. It perches quietly at length, swinging its tail like a pendulum. The Rufous Motmot feeds on fruit, insects, frogs and lizards and returns to a perch to feed. It has a loud bubbling, hooting call which is heard most often at dawn. It is commonly seen in the rain forests of the lowlands and foothills of the Caribbean slope.

BLUE-CROWNED MOTMOT *Momotus momota* 39cm (15.5in)

Both sexes of this species are alike with green upperparts, green-rufous underparts, a black mask and blue cap with black on the crown. They have a confiding nature and call with a soft double hoot 'hoop-hoop'. As with all motmots they perch in an upright position often swinging their long tail back and forward. The long central feathers and their racquet tips are conspicuous but can sometimes be missing. They utilize a range of habitats including rain forests, forest edges and plantations, mainly along the lowlands of the Pacific slope.

RUFOUS-TAILED JACAMAR *Galbula ruficauda* 23cm (9in)

This is an elegant bird with a lean, streamlined body from the tip of its long, fine bill to its slender tail. They have metallic green upperparts and this colour extends around to a green breast band, while belly and under the tail are rufous. The sexes are similar, differing only in the colour of the throat, white on the male and buff on the female. They forage along forest edges and in clearings for insects, particularly dragonflies and butterflies, including species as large as Morphos. Occurs along the Caribbean slope at low to mid altitudes and the southern part of the Pacific slope.

WHITE-WHISKERED PUFFBIRD *Malacoptila panamensis* 18cm (7in)

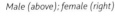

Male (above); female (right)

A stocky bird which often sits with its feathers fluffed out giving it the appearance of having a large head and short neck. This species has distinctive bristly white feathers forming a moustache; otherwise it is largely a streaked brown. Often seen in pairs, with the male more cinnamon than the female, which is greyer above with more white on the belly. Both sexes have a red eye. They are quiet forest birds that can be trusting when approached. They perch in shaded areas waiting for prey to pass. They occur at low altitudes on the Caribbean slope and also on the southern Pacific slope.

PRONG-BILLED BARBET *Semnornis frantzii* 17cm (6.75in)

This is a stout bird with a short but solid bill, slightly hooked at the tip. It is largely olive- or orange-brown with a small black mask. The male also has a black streak on the nape. Feeds mainly on fruits but supplements this diet with some insects and nectar. It congregates in small flocks except during the nesting season when it is territorial. Often heard giving a loud, conspicuous whooping 'wha-wha-wha' call. Inhabits humid forests including old secondary growth at mid-elevations on both slopes and is a regional endemic.

EMERALD TOUCANET *Aulacorhynchus prasinus* 29cm (11.5in)

This bird has the unmistakable outline of a toucan in spite of being much smaller than most in this group. It is mostly bright green with a blue throat and the large bill is yellow and black. Feeds mainly on fruit but is an opportunistic feeder which also takes insects, nestlings, small reptiles etc., for which it forages in small, loose flocks. It favours forest edges and semi-open habitats in middle and high forest areas throughout Costa Rica. Costa Rican birds are now usually considered to be Blue-throated Toucanet *A. caeruleogularis*, a separate species from the white-throated form.

COLLARED ARACARI *Pteroglossus torquatus* 41cm (16in)

This member of the toucan family has one of the less brightly coloured bills of the group with conspicuous heavy serrations on the upper mandible. Its plumage is mainly glossy black with brighter underparts, which are yellow tinged with red, and it has a dark band across its belly and a black spot on its breast. Generally seen in small, straggling flocks in the lowlands and foothills of the Caribbean slope, only rarely on the Pacific side. Replaced by the similar, but more brightly coloured, Fiery-billed Aracari (see below) on the south Pacific slope.

FIERY-BILLED ARACARI *Pteroglossus frantzii* 43cm (17in)

This species is similar to the related Collared Aracari (see above) but has a broader and brighter band across the belly and a larger breast spot. Its bill is more brightly coloured in brilliant orange-red but has only small serrations. It is seen in small flocks that forage at higher levels of trees for their diet of fruit, insects and nestlings. It inhabits the humid forests of the south Pacific slope up to altitudes of c.1500m which means its range does not overlap with that of the Collared Aracari. It is a regional endemic.

KEEL-BILLED TOUCAN *Ramphastos sulfuratus*
male 47cm (18.5in), female 44cm (17in)

This toucan has a flamboyant, rainbow-coloured bill. The sexes are similar, though the male is larger with a longer bill, and their plumage is mostly black with a bright yellow throat and chest. They travel about the canopy of lowland rain forests in small, noisy groups feeding mainly on fruit but also invertebrates and small reptiles. Their croaking, frog-like call is a characteristic sound of lowland rain forest in late afternoon. They are commonly found in forested lowlands on the Caribbean slope but are less numerous on the Pacific side.

CHESTNUT-MANDIBLED TOUCAN *Ramphastos swainsonii*
male 56cm (22in), female 52cm (20.5in)

The largest of the toucans to be found in Costa Rica, this species has a striking yellow and dark maroon bill. Its behaviour and habits are similar to that of the Keel-billed Toucan and they can often be found in the same areas competing for food. Most easily differentiated by their bill colours and calls. The Chestnut-mandibled's voice is shriller, more yelping, and it calls incessantly during the evening. It is common in the lowlands of the south Pacific slope (where Keel-billed is absent) as well as on the Caribbean slope.

ACORN WOODPECKER *Melanerpes formicivorus* 21cm (8.25in)

This species has a distinctive black, white and red facial-pattern. The back is black with a white rump and wing-patch and underparts white, streaked with black below the breast. The female has a black forehead. This is a social species that famously stores food for future use by using natural crevices or drilling holes for a larder. They feed on acorns, fruit and insects found in forests and their clearings and borders and also neighboring pastures. They are found in the highlands, chiefly from c.1500m to the tree line, of Cordilleras Central and Talamanca.

BLACK-CHEEKED WOODPECKER *Melanerpes pucherani* 18.5cm (7.25in)

A characteristic woodpecker showing the group's adaptations to feeding and nesting in tree trunks. It has a heavily barred black back and white rump. The male has a conspicuous red crown and nape while the female has black in the centre of its crown. A bird of humid forests, favouring the higher levels of trees, foraging for insects and eating more fruit than other woodpeckers. It occurs commonly in the lowlands on the Caribbean slope. Similar to the Golden-naped Woodpecker *Melanerpes chrysauchen*, which replaces it on the south Pacific slope.

HOFFMAN'S WOODPECKER *Melanerpes hoffmannii* 18cm (7in)

Male (above); female (right)

This species is heavily barred on the back and pale buffy-brown below but with yellow on the belly. The male has a red crown and yellow nape. The female is similar but lacks the red crown and has a smaller area of yellow on the nape. It inhabits the less dense woodlands of secondary forests, dry forests, plantations and gardens. Supplements its insect diet with fruits and nectar. Usually seen in pairs. Occurs commonly on north Pacific slopes but is expanding its range onto the Caribbean side. The similar Red-crowned Woodpecker *Melanerpes rubricapillus*, replaces it on the south Pacific slope.

HAIRY WOODPECKER *Picoides villosus* 17cm (6.75in)

Male (above); female (right)

One of the smaller woodpeckers with brown underparts and a black back with a broad conspicuous white stripe down the middle. The head is mostly black with white stripes above and below the eye. The male has a red patch on the back of the crown, lacking in the female. They forage for invertebrates mostly at mid-levels of trees in humid highland forests, but also at lower levels and on the ground. They inhabit forested highlands, particularly oak woodlands, between c.1500m to the tree line, from Cordillera de Tilarán south to Panama.

GOLDEN-OLIVE WOODPECKER *Piculus rubiginosus* 20cm (8in)

Male (left); female (right)

A largely olive-green bird which is heavily barred on its underparts. It has a grey face and a dark grey crown with bright red stripes. The sexes are similar but the female lacks the moustachial stripe. It can be difficult to spot as it forages for ants and termites in heavy foliage of the canopy, though it occasionally descends to lower levels. It often attracts attention by its loud rattling trill. It is widespread in mid-elevation wooded areas throughout Costa Rica.

LINEATED WOODPECKER *Dryocopus lineatus* 33cm (13in)

A striking woodpecker with black back and tail, buff underparts with dark barring and a conspicuous red, pointed crest. Two white stripes run from the base of the bill down the sides of the neck and back. The male has a red moustachial stripe which is lacking in the female and a more extensive red crest. They favour forest edges and semi-open habitats such as gardens and small patches of trees, and forage on trunks and branches for invertebrates and some fruit. Inhabit wooded lowlands on both slopes up to 1000m.

PALE-BILLED WOODPECKER *Campephilus guatemalensis*
37cm (14.5in)

A dark woodpecker with a red, crested head, strong barring on the underside and white stripes extending from the neck down the back where they meet to form a V. The female has black on the front of her head. They use their heavy bill for probing for their principle prey of beetles and grubs. This species is a resident of lowlands on both slopes where it forages mostly at mid and high levels of woodland and at edges of clearings. It is similar to Lineated Woodpecker (see opposite) but their head patterns differ.

WEDGE-BILLED WOODCREEPER *Glyphorhynchus spirurus*
15cm (6in)

A small, slender, tree climbing bird that forages over trunks and branches in search of insect prey. It has stiffened, spiny tail feathers to support it on trunks, and a short, laterally flattened and slightly upturned bill to facilitate probing for food items in bark and epiphytes. Its brown mottled colouring makes it inconspicuous and difficult to spot particularly when it remains still. All the woodcreepers have similar colouring which can make identification difficult. In this case, however, a combination of its size and the characteristically shaped bill is diagnostic. Occurs in forested lowlands and foothills on the Caribbean slope and the southern part of the Pacific slope.

BARRED WOODCREEPER *Dendrocolaptes certhia* 28cm (11in)

One of the larger woodcreepers and strongly barred over most of its body. It is the only one of this group with barring on its upperparts. It has a substantial dark bill and prefers foraging in low and middle levels of trees as well as in association with army ants on or near the ground. Has a variety of loud calls heard mostly at dawn and dusk. It occurs commonly in lowlands up to mid-elevations on both slopes but is rarer in dry areas of the northwest.

BUFF-THROATED WOODCREEPER *Xiphorhynchus guttatus* 21.5cm (8.5in)

A typical woodcreeper with rufous wings and tail, buff body with darker streaks, streaked on head with a pale stripe behind the eye. Throat is pale buff with a fine black moustachial stripe and a substantial dark bill. The straight, dark bill differentiates it from other woodcreepers with buff throats. Forages for small invertebrates, probing in bark and epiphytes as it ascends trunks from a low level, also along branches. Generally alone but sometimes in mixed flocks. Prefers humid forest edges and clearings in the lowlands of the Caribbean slope to c.650m and slightly higher on the south Pacific slope. Now designated as Cocoa Woodcreeper *X. susurrans*.

BLACK-STRIPED WOODCREEPER *Xiphorhynchus lachrymosus*
24cm (9.5in)

This species has plain rufous flight feathers and tail but the rest of the body is boldly patterned with black edging to the buff feathers giving a spotted and streaked effect. The bill is straight, laterally-compressed and substantial. As is characteristic of woodcreepers it forages over bark and epiphytes but favours higher levels of trees than most of its relatives. It preys mostly on invertebrates but occasionally takes small reptiles and often joins mixed flocks when foraging. It inhabits wet forests in lowlands of the Caribbean and south Pacific slopes.

SPOTTED WOODCREEPER *Xiphorhynchus erythropygius*
23cm (9in)

This species has the rufous wings and stiff, rufous tail common to most woodcreepers but the rest of its plumage is olive-brown and with a distinctive spotted pattern particularly on the underparts. The bill is straight, long and darker on the upper mandible than on the lower. Although it forages on trunks, it favours branches and can be acrobatic in its search for invertebrates and other small prey. It has a melancholy sounding call of two to three clear whistles. It inhabits humid forests and prefers the mid-elevations of mountainous areas on both slopes.

STREAKED-HEADED WOODCREEPER
Lepidocolaptes souleyetii 19cm (7.5in)

This is a slim, streaked woodcreeper with a slightly down-curved bill. It has rufous wings and tail, a buff throat, and buff streaking edged with black on the underparts and upper back. The top of the head has fine buff streaks. Clings to bark in the usual woodcreeper fashion and hitches up trunks and along branches probing for invertebrates. It prefers less dense woodlands, plantations and areas with scattered trees in the lowlands of both slopes up to c.1500m but is rarer in the dry northwest.

STREAKED-BREASTED TREEHUNTER
Thripadectes rufobrunneus 21.5cm (8.5in)

This species is largely rufous-brown with a darker mottled head, a distinctive buff throat and buff streaking on its breast. It has a relatively heavy, dark bill and lacks any streaking on its back. It feeds on invertebrates and occasional small reptiles and amphibians. It forages actively, poking around in epiphytes and tangled vegetation in the heavy undergrowth of highland forests. It favours cool, humid cloud forests in the mountains the length of the country. A regional endemic.

BUFF-THROATED FOLIAGE-GLEANER
Automolus ochrolaemus 18.5cm (7.25in)

This species has olive-brown upperparts, plain yellow-brown underparts with conspicuous buffy throat and 'spectacles'. It forages in the lower levels of humid forests including secondary growth and plantations when they are old and correspondingly dense, occasionally descending to the ground. Feeds on invertebrates and small amphibians and reptiles. Occurs in the lowlands and foothills of the Caribbean and south Pacific slopes. Also known as Buff-throated Automolus.

GREY-THROATED LEAFTOSSER *Sclerurus albigularis* 17cm (6.75in)

This is a ground-dwelling bird that forages on the forest floor, tossing aside leaflitter and probing damp soil in its search for invertebrates. They have dark brown back and wings, a black tail, a chestnut chest and rump and a grey throat. The earthy colours of their plumage make them rather inconspicuous though they are not particularly shy. Can often be seen on forest trails at dawn and dusk. The grey throat patch distinguishes this species from the similar Tawny-throated Leaftosser *Sclerurus mexicanus*. Most likely to be found at mid-elevations on the Caribbean slope but their range spills over to the north cordilleras of the Pacific slope.

77

PLAIN XENOPS *Xenops minutus* 12cm (4.75in)

This acrobatic forager is small and brown but with a conspicuous silvery-white cheek-stripe and a less distinct pale stripe over the eye. It has dark bars on the wings and tail. The lower mandible of its bill is curved upwards giving the whole beak the appearance of being tilted upwards. It sidles and hitches around the lower and mid levels of trees in search of its invertebrate prey, often as part of a mixed flock. It inhabits the lowlands and foothills on both slopes but is rare in the drier regions of the northwest. It is more uniform than the Streaked Xenops *X. rutilans* but their ranges rarely overlap.

FASCIATED ANTSHRIKE *Cymbilaimus lineatus* 18cm (7in)

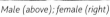

Male (above); female (right)

The male is finely barred in black and white over all its plumage except for its cap, which is black. The female is similar but in shades of brown. Both sexes have a hook-tipped and robust bill. They favour dense thickets, especially along streams and forest edges, so can be difficult to see. They do not appear very active in their foraging habits in the low to middle heights of the trees of lowland rain forests on the Caribbean slope. The male Barred Antshrike *Thamnophilus doliatus* is similar but prefers dense secondary thickets and dry forests.

BLACK-HOODED ANTSHRIKE *Thamnophilus bridgesi*
16.5cm (6.5in)

Male (above); female (right)

The male is almost entirely black, fading to slate-grey on lower underparts with white spots on the wings. The female is more olive-brown and streaked on head, throat and breast. They are often found as pairs and can be difficult to see in the dense thickets and tangled growth they prefer but often easier to observe than other antshrikes. Occur commonly in the lowlands and foothills of the southern Pacific humid forests. The male need not be confused with the male Slaty Antshrike *Thamnophilus punctatus* as their ranges do not overlap. The male is larger and darker than the male Dusky Antbird (see p80). An area endemic.

PLAIN ANTVIREO *Dysithamnus mentalis* 11.5cm (4.5in)

Male on nest (above); female (right)

The male is largely grey with a darker head, narrow white stripes on the wing and paler underparts becoming pale yellow on the belly and under the tail. The female is olive-brown above, lacking wing stripes, rufous on top of the head and with a pale eye-ring. Underparts are buffy yellow, palest at the throat. A bird usually seen in pairs or family groups, which forages rather deliberately in the understorey of humid forests gleaning invertebrates. It inhabits the middle elevations of the Caribbean slope and the south Pacific slope.

SLATY ANTWREN *Myrmotherula schisticolor* 10cm (4in)

Male (above); female (below)

The male is dark slate grey with black on the throat and chest and with narrow white wing bars. The female lacks the wing bars and is olive-brown above and a paler and brighter brown below. They usually forage as a pair in the middle levels of the understorey of forests, and also join mixed flocks. Appear busy as they probe rolled leaves and clumps of dead vegetation for small insects. They inhabit the wet forested areas of mid-elevations on both slopes.

DUSKY ANTBIRD *Cercomacra tyrannina* 14.5cm (5.75in)

The male is a slaty-grey to black bird with faint white barring on the wings and white tips to the tail feathers. The female is brown above and rufous below. Their slender bills are tipped with a small hook. They forage as a pair in dense thickets and undergrowth at forest edges. They are common in the rain forests of the lowlands and foothills on both slopes. This species is similar to the Slaty Antshrike *Thamnophilus punctatus* but is smaller, has a smaller and thinner bill and much less white on the wings.

Male (above); female (below)

CHESTNUT-BACKED ANTBIRD *Myrmeciza exsul* 14cm (5.5in)

The male is chestnut brown above with a black head and underparts while the female is chestnut brown with black largely confined to the head. Both have a heavy bill, a short tail and a conspicuous area of bare blue skin around the eye. They skulk in thickets and shaded areas but they respond easily to imitations of their whistles of 'come-here' or 'quick-come-here'. They forage for invertebrates in the dense undergrowth of lowland forests. The Immaculate Antbird *Myrmeciza immaculata* is larger, darker and with a proportionately longer tail. The Dull-mantled Antbird *Myrmeciza laemosticta* lacks the blue orbital patch and has spotted wing bars.

Male (above); female (below)

SPECTACLED ANTPITTA *Hylopezus perspicillatus* 12.5cm (5in)

This is a terrestrial bird of rain forests. Its streaked breast and pale broad eye-ring are conspicuous in the field. It has a grey cap and the olive-brown back and wings are lightly streaked and spotted in buff. Its long legs, very short tail and rotund body give it the distinctive outline of all antpittas. It has a springy hop and prefers the more open forest floor for foraging for invertebrates, which it does alone. It inhabits the lowlands and foothills on the Caribbean slope and the south Pacific slope. Also named Streak-chested Antpitta and sometimes placed in the genus *Grallaria*.

CINNAMON BECARD *Pachyramphus cinnamomeus* 14cm (5.5in)

An all-rufous bird but with paler underparts, especially at the throat, and a pale stripe above the eye. Unusually in this group, both males and females are the same. It is superficially similar to the Rufous Mourner (see p.92) and Rufous Piha *Lipaugus unirufus*, but is smaller and with less uniform colouring. This species prefers relatively open habitats such as forest edges and along streams. It has a frequently uttered, plaintive, piping call. It is common on the Caribbean slope up to foothills, but much rarer on the Pacific side.

WHITE-WINGED BECARD *Pachyramphus polychopterus* 14.5cm (5.75in)

Male (above); female (right)

The illustrations show the relatively large head and thick bill characteristic of this group. The male is black and grey with white markings on the wing. The female is olive-green above, buff below, with buff markings on her wings, a pale throat and a pale eye-ring. This species favours lightly-wooded areas where it forages at mid to high levels of trees for small invertebrates and fruits. Found in the lowlands of both slopes but are least numerous in dry areas.

MASKED TITYRA *Tityra semifasciata* 21cm (8.25in)

Male (above); female (right)

This is a striking bird, largely greyish-white with black on the face, wings and tail. The female is tinged with pale buffy-brown and has a brown mask and cap. Both have bare red skin at the base of the bill and around the eye. Their calls are strange grunting croaks. Feed on fruit with invertebrates and small reptiles gleaned from the canopy at forest edges and clearings. It is common up to mid-elevations on both slopes. The Black-crowned Tityra *Tityra inquisitor* is similar but lacks any bare red skin.

BARE-NECKED UMBRELLABIRD *Cephalopterus glabricollis*
male 41cm (16in) female 36cm (14in)

The male is all-black except for his red throat-sac and wattle and he has a conspicuous, umbrella-shaped crest. The female is a duller black with a smaller crest. The male displays by erecting his crest, inflating his throat-sac, and making a hooting call that sounds like blowing over a half-empty bottle. Mostly inhabits the lower canopy and mid-layers of primary forests and feeds on fruit supplemented with frogs, lizards and large insects. Has an unusual outline in flight created by its broad wings, short tail and crested head. Breeds at mid-elevations on the Caribbean slope but descends to lowlands at other times of year, where it is seen more easily e.g. La Selva Biological Station.

THREE-WATTLED BELLBIRD *Procnias tricarunculata*
male 30cm (12in), female 25cm (10in)

Male (above); female (right)

The male is renowned for its huge gape, which is adorned with three wattles, and its loud calls. He has a chestnut body and white head and neck while the female has olive-green upper parts and is yellow below streaked with olive. Bellbirds are specialist fruit eaters so can be erratic in their movements depending on the availability of fruit. They breed in highlands and move to lower altitudes at other times of the year when they are liable to turn up anywhere there is a suitable food source.

RED-CAPPED MANAKIN *Pipra mentalis* 10cm (4in)

The male has a black body, scarlet head, and yellow thighs, a distinctive plumage that he shows off when displaying. The female, on the other hand, is a pale olive-green in common with several other female manakins. During an entertaining courtship several males gather in a dispersed lek and display to attract females. They are small, active birds that eat mainly fruit and forage in the lower and middle levels of forests. They are common in the lowlands on the Caribbean slope and in the south on the Pacific slope.

BLUE-CROWNED MANAKIN *Pipra coronata* 9cm (3.5in)

Male (above); female (right)

Although tiny, the largely black male is easily identified by his bright blue cap. The mostly green female, however, is difficult to differentiate from many other female manakins though she is brighter green with less olive on her back, paler below. They prefer forest with little undergrowth where they forage for small insects and berries. Likely to be seen alone except at leks. The courtship display is less elaborate with none of the mechanical wing snapping noises of other manakins. They are found in low and mid-elevations on the southern Pacific slope.

LONG-TAILED MANAKIN *Chiroxiphia linearis* 11.5cm (4.5in)

The male is a striking if diminutive bird with his sky blue back, scarlet cap, orange legs and elongated central tail feathers. The female does not possess such finery being a fairly uniform olive-green though paler below. Her central tail feathers extend a mere inch or so but this aids differentiating her from other female manakins. Young males look similar to females and moult gradually into mature plumage over 3–4 years, so are often seen in intermediate regalia. Two to three males display in leks during the breeding season. They inhabit the undergrowth of woodland at low to mid-elevations of the northern Pacific slope.

ORANGE-COLLARED MANAKIN *Manacus aurantiacus*
10cm (4in)

Male (above); female (right)

The glossy, orange collar below a black cap give this male a distinctive appearance. The photograph also shows the modified primaries that are narrowed and bent so they can produce loud snapping noises during courtship displays. The female is olive- green, slightly darker on the head and more yellow on the lower belly and, like the male, has orange legs. She resembles the female White-collared Manakin (see below) but their ranges do not overlap. This species favours the more open areas of the understorey of rain forests on the southern Pacific slope. An area endemic.

WHITE-COLLARED MANAKIN *Manacus candei* 11cm (4.25in)

The male alone has a broad white collar which extends down onto his back. He has a black cap, wings and lower back, green rump and yellow belly making him much more distinctive than the olive- green female. The female can be distinguished from most other female manakins by the yellow on her lower belly and orange legs. She resembles the Orange-collared female (see above) but their ranges do not overlap. During courtship males clear an area of forest floor for their leaping and wing snapping displays. This species favours dense vegetation of humid forests on the Caribbean slope.

SCISSOR-TAILED FLYCATCHER *Tyrannus forficatus* 19.5cm
(7.75in), plus 15cm (6in) male, 9cm (3.5in) female, for tail feathers

This elegant bird is silver-grey above with dark wings, a blush of pink on its back and belly and a white breast. It has a salmon pink patch under its wing visible only in flight. Its most striking feature is its hugely elongated tail, only slightly shorter in the female. It perches for long periods, often on fencing, while waiting for prey for which it makes swift, dashing forays. It hunts its insect prey in open, savannah type areas and also eats some berries. Roosts communally. It is a common winter resident in the dry northwest Pacific slope but may be seen elsewhere when the resident population is supplemented by migrating birds.

TROPICAL KINGBIRD *Tyrannus melancholicus* 21cm (8.25in)

This species has yellow underparts tinged with grey on the breast and a grey-olive back. It has an all dark notched tail, large bill and an orangey-red patch on the crown, concealed except when the bird is excited. Males and females have the same plumage. This species perches in open places ready to pursue insect prey with often impressive aerial acrobatics. It is common throughout the country up to altitudes of c.2000m, scarcer at higher altitudes. Seen readily on utility wires and fences. The similar Western Kingbird *T. verticalis* is a migrant visitor from North America which generally occurs on the Pacific slope, mainly at Guanacaste. It can be differentiated by its less distinct dark mask and squarer tail with white outer tail feathers.

WHITE-RINGED FLYCATCHER *Coryphotriccus albovittatus*
16cm (6.25in)

This yellow-bellied flycatcher is very similar to Social Flycatcher (see p91) but it has a more boldly patterned head and a longer bill. A broad white stripe runs from the base of the bill, above the eye and meets at the nape. The yellow crown patch can be either concealed in the black cap or visible. It forages in small groups, sallying from perches in tall trees after insects. It also takes berries. It inhabits the lowlands of the Caribbean slope occasionally reaching foothills.

BOAT-BILLED FLYCATCHER *Megarhynchus pitangua* 23cm (9in)

This is one of several flycatchers with black and white head patterns. It has a powerful bill, and is yellow below, olive above and has a dark head with a conspicuous white stripe above the eye, a white throat and a usually concealed orange crown patch. It favours forest edges, particularly along rivers and eats fruit and large insects by sallying and gleaning. It is common throughout Costa Rica up to altitudes of c.1800m. It is more olive than the similar Great Kiskadee (see p.92), lacks its rufous wing panel and has a larger bill.

BRIGHT-RUMPED ATTILA *Attila spadiceus* 18cm (7in)

This species has very variable colouring ranging through olive-green to brown-green and with differing amounts of yellow and streaking, but they all have the same general appearance. It has a proportionately large head with a substantial bill, hooked at the tip and usually has a yellow rump and streaked underparts. It has a very upright stance and frequently lifts its tail up and down. It's an active, noisy bird, foraging at many levels in forests in search of its varied diet. It inhabits both wet and dry forests throughout the country except at the highest altitudes.

SULPHUR-BELLIED FLYCATCHER *Myiodynastes luteiventris* 20cm (8in)

This is a heavily streaked bird with a rufous rump and tail. It has a heavy black stripe through the eye and a fine one below it, and a white throat above yellow, darkly streaked underparts. It closely resembles Streaked Flycatcher (see p.90) but has a heavier moustachial stripe and the yellow on underparts extends further down the belly. It sounds peevish when calling, forages for insects and berries in drier forests and fairly open areas. It is a breeding resident in the north, but can be seen throughout low and middle altitudes as a passage migrant in spring and autumn.

89

STREAKED FLYCATCHER *Myiodynastes maculatus* 20cm (8in)

This flycatcher has a rufous rump and tail, buff back and wings and white to pale yellow underparts. There is black streaking on the head, back and breast. The head has a conspicuous black mask edged with white below, and a dark moustachial stripe. The bill is heavy, with a dark upper mandible and a small hooked tip. It hawks and sallies for insects in clearings and edges of woodland and open areas with some trees. It is a resident of lowlands on the Pacific slope and also a passage migrant. Closely resembles Sulphur-bellied Flycatcher (see p.89).

GOLDEN-BELLIED FLYCATCHER *Myiodynastes hemichrysus* 20cm (8in)

This species is yellow below, dark olive above and has a white stripe both above and below its eye, a black stripe through the eye, plus a grey moustachial stripe. The head pattern distinguishes this species from other flycatchers with yellow bellies. Occurs in pairs and family parties made conspicuous by their noisy habits in gaps and edges of cloud forests. Perches upright at mid to high positions of a tree from which it can fly out in pursuit of its insect prey. A resident of the Caribbean slope for the length of the country but is less widespread on the Pacific slope and is a regional endemic.

GREY-CAPPED FLYCATCHER *Myiozetetes granadensis*
16.5cm (6.5in)

This species has a shorter bill than most other yellow-bellied flycatchers. Its back is olive-green and wings and tail are dark cinnamon. It resembles Social Flycatcher (see below), and can often be seen with it, but white on the head is restricted to the forehead and extends back only as a small indistinct stripe above the eye. There is a vermilion crown patch, which is usually concealed, and reduced in females. It can often be seen in family groups or small flocks and prefers open shrubby land. Occurs commonly in the lowlands up to c.1600m of the Caribbean slope and south Pacific slope.

SOCIAL FLYCATCHER *Myiozetetes similis* 16cm (6.25in)

Another yellow-bellied flycatcher with a black-and-white head pattern. It also has an orange-red crown patch which is generally concealed. Its conspicuous eyestripe distinguishes it from Grey-capped Flycatcher (see above) and it has a smaller bill than White-ringed Flycatcher (see page 88). It favours clearings, fields and gardens where it forages for invertebrates and fruit. It is resident and common throughout the country except at very high elevations. Also known as Vermillion-crowned Flycatcher.

GREAT KISKADEE *Pitangus sulphuratus* 23cm (9in)

This species is one of the largest of the flycatchers. It is brown above and yellow below with a bold white throat and stripe above the eye. It has an obscured yellow cap which it displays more frequently than other flycatchers. It is noisy (kiskadee reflecting its call) and an opportunist feeder. Feeds predominantly on invertebrates but will also take berries and other prey, even diving for small fish and tadpoles. It is easy to see in open habitats of the lowlands and up to mid-elevation throughout the country. The Boat-billed Flycatcher is similar but more olive on its back, has a heavier bill and lacks the rufous in the wing.

RUFOUS MOURNER *Rhytipterna holerythra* 20cm (8in)

This flycatcher is rufous-brown all over though paler on the underparts and darker on the wings. The bill is pale at the base and dark at the tip. It sallies and gleans for insects and fruit at middle or upper tree levels and often joins mixed species flocks. Its call is a mournful wolf whistle. It inhabits humid woodland including rain forest and plantations up to c.1200m on the Caribbean and south Pacific slopes. The similar Rufous Piha *Lipaugus unirufus* is distinctly larger and has a different call.

BROWN-CRESTED FLYCATCHER *Myiarchus tyrannulus*
19cm (7.5in)

This flycatcher is grey-brown on its back, has rufous on wings and tail and pale yellow underparts. There are two wing bars. The bill is all black which is helpful in differentiating this species from the similar Great-crested Flycatcher *Myiarchus crinitus*. Brown-crested Flycatchers forage around middle levels of trees in fairly open country and feed on insects and berries. They have a habit of bobbing like a lizard when disturbed. They inhabit the lowlands and foothills of the drier northern parts of the Pacific slope.

DUSKY-CAPPED FLYCATCHER *Myiarchus tuberculifer*
16.5cm (6.5in)

A flycatcher with yellow and grey below, largely olive above but with rufous on wings and tail, and has a blackish, dusky cap. Related flycatchers have similar plumage colours but lack the contrasting dark cap. It has the typical flycatcher habit of catching prey in flight and inhabits wooded areas with clearings and gaps. It is common and found throughout the country up to an altitude of c.1200m.

WESTERN WOOD-PEWEE *Contopus sordidulus* 14cm (5.5in)

This is a grey bird with dark grey wings apart from the pale wing bars, a dusky head and paler grey below. It is so similar to the Eastern Wood-Pewee *C. virens* that it may not be possible to differentiate between the two unless their calls are heard when the Western Wood-Pewee sounds hoarser and more nasal than the clear whistle of the Eastern. Hunts flying insects in typical flycatcher fashion. Seen in spring and autumn as a passage migrant on both slopes, most commonly between 700–3000m whilst Eastern Wood-Pewee tends to prefer the lower altitudes upto c.1500m.

YELLOW-BELLIED FLYCATCHER *Empidonax flaviventris* 12cm (4.75in)

This small flycatcher is greenish on its back, olive to yellow on its chest and throat and with a yellow belly. It has a pale eye-ring and two pale wing-bars. This species is a winter visitor that favours the understorey of forests though it forages in a wider range of habitats when migrating through the country. They are seen as migrants along both slopes up to mid-elevations but winter residents tend to prefer the lowlands of both slopes. Difficult to distinguish from several other *Empidonax* flycatchers.

94

YELLOWISH FLYCATCHER *Empidonax flavescens* 12.5cm (5in)

One of the small flycatchers, this species is olive above, yellow-olive below, with a conspicuous pale eye-ring and two darker yellowish wing bars. It is brighter with a more obvious eye-ring than similar related flycatchers. It perches in the understorey from which it sallies for insects in typical flycatcher fashion, but also gleans from foliage and eats some berries. It is a resident of the cool forests between c.800–2000m on both slopes though tends to go higher on the Pacific side.

BLACK-CAPPED FLYCATCHER *Empidonax atriceps* 11.5cm (4.5in)

This is a small flycatcher with a dark olive-brown back and black on the head but paler below. Its pale eye-ring shows up well below the black cap though it is incomplete. This is a bird of the highlands, preferring montane oak forests and surrounding areas. It sallies to catch flying insects in typical flycatcher fashion, mainly in the upper part of the canopy. Occurs in the highlands of Cordillera Central and Cordillera de Talamanca. An area endemic.

TUFTED FLYCATCHER *Mitrephanes phaeocercus* 12cm (4.75in)

This is a small flycatcher with a distinctive pointed crest. It is olive-green above with two buff wing-bars and rich ochre below becoming yellow on the lower belly. A bird of dense highland forests, foraging in clearings and at edges. It sallies from a perch to catch insects and on returning gives a characteristic quiver of its tail. Inhabits the highlands of both slopes between altitudes of 700–3000m but is most common in the middle of that range.

WHITE-THROATED SPADEBILL *Platyrinchus mystaceus* 9.5cm (3.75in)

This is a very small flycatcher with a short tail and a distinctive facial pattern but its most obvious feature is its flat and very broad bill. It is largely brown though paler below with a usually concealed bright yellow crown. Forages in the shady forest understorey so can be difficult to see. Occurs at mid-elevations on both the Caribbean and Pacific slopes. It is replaced by the very similar Stub-tailed Spadebill *Platyrinchus cancrominus* in dry Pacific lowlands.

YELLOW-OLIVE FLYCATCHER *Tolmomyias sulphurescens*
13cm (5in)

This species has an olive-green back and grey head with pale, narrow eye-rings that extend to the rather flat bill, giving it a 'spectacled' look. The throat is pale grey and the belly pale yellow. The dusky wing feathers are edged in yellow. It occurs in both dry and humid wooded areas including secondary growth, pastures and gardens and feeds mainly on insects with some berries also. Although it can be seen in the lowlands of the Caribbean slope it is most abundant in the Pacific lowlands and foothills.

COMMON TODY-FLYCATCHER *Todirostrum cinereum*
9.5cm (3.75in)

This is a tiny flycatcher with a large, flat and broad bill, entirely yellow underparts, a slaty grey back and black wing feathers with yellow edges. It can be distinguished from Black-headed Tody-Flycatcher *T. nigriceps* by its conspicuous yellow eye and grey back. When foraging for insects, frequently in pairs, they flick and wag their tails. This species can be found in areas with shrubs and small trees throughout the country at altitudes below 1500m.

YELLOW-BELLIED ELAENIA *Elaenia flavogaster* 15cm (6in)

This species has olive-brown upperparts, a pale grey throat merging into the yellow of its belly and two buff wing bars. It has narrow pale eye-rings and an untidy crest with an inconspicuous white crown patch. An active bird, usually seen in pairs. Feeds on insects, small fruit and berries. It prefers open, scrubby habitats so is extending its range into deforested areas. It can be found in lowlands and foothills on both slopes. It is similar to Lesser Elaenia *Elaenia chiriquensis* but bigger, with a larger crest.

MOUNTAIN ELAENIA *Elaenia frantzii* 15cm (6in)

This elaenia is greenish brown above and pale yellow-olive below. The wings are slightly darker than the back and have a double wing bar and white edging to some wing feathers giving pale patches when the wings are folded. It has a narrow pale eye-ring and a bushy top to the head but no crest or crown patch. It forages alone in the canopy of trees at edges and clearings of highland forests and feeds on both insects and fruits. Occurs in highlands throughout the country only occasionally descending to elevations below 1200m. Its lack of crest and crown patch, and preference for highlands, differentiate it from other elaenias.

MISTLETOE TYRANNULET *Zimmerius vilissimus* 9.5cm (3.75in)

This flycatcher is olive above, streaked grey below, with conspicuous yellow edging to its wing feathers. Its head is grey with a paler stripe over the eye and it has a small bill. It is named for its liking for mistletoe berries, though it also feeds on other berries and small invertebrates. It is very small and active, flitting about in search of food. It occurs in any humid areas with mistletoe so can be found throughout most of the country. Often known as Paltry Tyrannulet.

BLUE-AND-WHITE SWALLOW *Notiochelidon cyanoleuca* 11cm (4.25in)

As its name implies this swallow is blue and white with the blue darkening to black on the wings and tail. It is one of the smallest swallows seen in Costa Rica and has a short, notched tail and relatively short wings. In flight it is most easily differentiated from other small swallows by its dark undertail coverts. Typical of swallows, this species hawks for insects on the wing. It is also often seen perched on overhead wires. It is common over inhabited areas and prefers mid to high elevations throughout the country.

MANGROVE SWALLOW *Tachycineta albilinea* 13cm (5in)

This is a small swallow, dark green above with a white stripe from base of bill to eye, white underparts and rump. Like all swallows it is streamlined and aerial and hawks for insects on the wing. It catches insects mostly low over open water so frequents habitats such as lakes, estuaries and mangroves and occasionally adjoining meadows. It is gregarious and flocks can often be seen perched close to their favoured feeding sites. They inhabit suitable areas in the lowlands of both slopes and occasionally up to c.1000m.

WHITE-THROATED MAGPIE-JAY *Calocitta formosa* 46cm (18in)

This bird is large, noisy, aggressive and unmistakable with its blue and white plumage, long, graduated tail and curled crest. It is a bird of dry forests and savannah areas where there are substantial numbers of trees. It occurs in small flocks which forage in search of a wide variety of food including invertebrates, small reptiles, amphibians, birds, fruit and nectar. It is common in the lower altitudes of the north Pacific slope and its range is gradually spreading south, now at least as far as Uvita.

BROWN JAY *Cyanocorax morio* 39cm (15.5in)

This is a large, raucous bird which is generally seen in small, noisy groups. It is mostly brown but with a cream to white belly and white tips to its outer tail feathers. It is an opportunistic feeder, taking more or less anything edible that it can find and is extremely social, including co-operative breeding. It inhabits open areas of scrub, woodland, plantations and deforested land and forages at all levels from the ground to tree tops. It can be found in most areas of Costa Rica up to an altitude of c.2500m.

AZURE-HOODED JAY *Cyanolyca cucullata* 29cm (11.5in)

This jay is dark blue with a black head and neck that is capped with a sky blue patch on its crown and nape which is bordered in white at its front edge. It forages in pairs or small groups through the middle layers of humid forests, searching actively for invertebrates and fruits amongst foliage, bark and epiphytes. It is widespread but not numerous at mid-elevations on both slopes, chiefly from Cordillera de Tilarán south to Panama.

BANDED-BACKED WREN *Campylorhynchus zonatus*
16.5cm (6.5in)

This is a large wren with heavy black and white barring on the back and dark spots on the underside. It has a long tail and a long, slightly down-curved bill. These conspicuous features make it difficult to confuse with other species. Family groups often forage among the foliage of clearings and forest edges in their agile search for their insect food. They have a harsh, grating call. They are commonly found on the Caribbean slope up to mid-elevations.

RUFOUS-NAPED WREN *Campylorhynchus rufinucha*
17cm (6.75in)

A large wren, which is white below, barred above, with a striking black cap, white stripe above the eye, a rufous nape and a relatively large, down-curved bill. It is insectivorous and forages in small, family groups among foliage of open woodland, including secondary growth and inhabited areas. Groups keep in contact with regular short rasping calls but mates have a melodious song sung as a duet. They occur in the dry lowlands of the north Pacific slope.

STRIPED-BREASTED WREN *Thryothorus thoracicus*
11.5cm (4.5in)

This small bird's most distinguishing feature is the white underparts heavily streaked with black. It is the only wren with these stripes as opposed to barring or spotting on underparts. Otherwise it is brown with heavy barring on the darker wings and tail. It has a long white stripe above the eye. It favours undergrowth in forest clearings and edges where it gleans actively among foliage. Commonly found in the lowlands the length of the Caribbean slope.

BAY WREN *Thryothorus nigricapillus* 14.5cm (5.75in)

This wren is mostly rich chestnut, black on its tail and wings. There is faint barring on the flanks of young birds (as shown). Its head is black with conspicuous white markings and with a white throat. Favours dense thickets and undergrowth, often bordering streams and pools, so can be difficult to see. It is very vocal and attracts attention with its loud whistles. It feeds on small invertebrates. Common and widespread in the lowlands of the Caribbean slope, less common in the drier most northerly area.

RIVERSIDE WREN *Thryothorus semibadius* 13cm (5in)

As shown, the undersides of this wren are finely barred in black on white while the upperparts are bright chestnut. The wings and tail are also barred. Like many wrens this species probes and gleans actively in dense thickets and undergrowth particularly favouring those alongside water. It has very varied calls and songs often sung as duets between pairs. It can be found on the south Pacific slope in the lowlands and up to c.1200m. It replaces the closely related Bay Wren (see p.103) on the Pacific slope south of Río Tarcoles.

HOUSE WREN *Troglodytes aedon* 10cm (4in)

This is a small, brown wren lacking in any strong markings. The wings and upper tail are barred and the belly and a stripe above the eye are a pale buff. Common in most areas of the county including around habitation and often roosts and nests in crevices in buildings. It is smaller, and has less clearly defined markings, than the Plain Wren *Thryothorus modestus* and has paler, less rich colouring than the smaller Ochraceous Wren *Troglodytes ochraceus*. The House Wren can be found throughout the country except at very high elevations.

GREY-BREASTED WOOD-WREN *Henicorhina leucophrys*
11cm (4.25in)

A small, plump bird which has a short, frequently cocked tail. It has brown upperparts, a grey breast, a dark grey cap and streaking on the face below a white stripe above the eye. It forages among low, dense vegetation but can be inquisitive so can be seen with patience. It has a loud, conspicuous song, frequently sung as a duet during the breeding season. It inhabits the highlands of both slopes. The similar but White-breasted Wood-Wren *Henicorhina leucosticta* is a bird of the lowlands. Where there is overlap at mid-elevations it can be differentiated by its white breast.

WHITE-THROATED ROBIN *Turdus assimilis* 22cm (8.75in)

This species is dark above, paler below with a bright yellow eye-ring and dull yellow bill and legs. It is distinguished from other thrushes by its white chin streaked with black and unmarked white upper breast. Largely arboreal but also forages for invertebrates and fruit on the ground and has a beautiful song. Inhabits humid forests and their edges, mainly on the Pacific slope, breeding on the lower slopes of highlands between c.800–1800m but descends to lower elevations at other times of the year.

CLAY-COLOURED ROBIN *Turdus grayi* 23.5cm (9.25in)

This species is a rather uniformly coloured warm brown thrush. Its dull brown plumage is relieved only by darker streaking on the throat, a yellow bill and a red-brown iris. The Mountain Robin is similar (see below) but is a greyer brown and has a black bill and dark iris and the two occur at different elevations. The Clay-coloured Robin has a beautiful song and can be found in cultivated and open areas throughout the country except in very dry or high places. It is the national bird of Costa Rica where it is called Yigüirro.

MOUNTAIN ROBIN *Turdus plebejus* 24cm (9.5in)

A brown-grey bird that is darker on the upperparts with indistinct streaking on the throat. Legs, eyes and bill are black. Generally a rather nondescript bird with a nondescript song compared with other thrushes, two monotonous alternating notes. It inhabits mountain forests where it forages for seeds, berries and invertebrates, both in trees and on the ground. It is common in highlands throughout the country at altitudes between c.1300m and the tree line, and descends to c.900m after the breeding season when it is most likely to be seen in flocks.

SOOTY ROBIN *Turdus nigrescens* 25.5cm (10in)

This robin has a blackish body with the sides of its face, wings and tail black. Its legs and bill are orange-yellow and the iris is pale grey. The male is shown above, the female similar but paler and browner. It prefers open ground at high elevations and generally forages on the ground for insects and berries. It is commonly found above 2500m in Cordillera Central and Cordillera de Talamanca but occasionally descends lower after the breeding season. The Mountain Robin (see opposite) is similar but smaller, duller and lacking the bright legs and bill.

BLACK-FACED SOLITAIRE *Myadestes melanops* 17cm (6.75in)

This is a slaty-grey bird with rather short legs, which perches in an upright position. It has a black mask, an orange bill and largely black wings and tail. It feeds chiefly on fruit and seeds. It has a beautiful, flutey song which has made it a target of the cage bird trade. It breeds in highlands and some of the population migrate to lower elevations in the non-breeding season. It inhabits thick undergrowth and the canopy in high, wet forests the length of the Caribbean and Pacific slopes and is an endemic of the Costa Rica/Chiriqui highlands region.

107

SLATY-BACKED NIGHTINGALE-THRUSH *Catharus fuscater*
17cm (6.75in)

Mostly very dark slaty-grey with a paler belly and a characteristic pale iris. This sombre colouring is brightened by an orange bill, eye-ring and legs. The Black-headed Nightingale-Thrush *Catharus mexicanus* can be distinguished by its less uniform colouring, browner on the back, with a pale chin and throat, and a dark eye. The Slaty-backed Nightingale-Thrush is chiefly a ground-dwelling bird, where it forages for insects and berries, and often attends ant swarms above 1500m where there are few professional ant followers. It inhabits forests between 800–2000m, mostly on the Caribbean slope.

BLACK-BILLED NIGHTINGALE-THRUSH *Catharus gracilirostris*
14.5cm (5.75in)

This is the smallest of the nightingale-thrushes and the only one with dark bill and legs. It is grey over most of its underparts but the olive-brown of its back is repeated as a band across the breast. It frequents oak forests of higher elevations and more open areas in these surroundings such as pastures and gardens. It forages on the ground and up into the canopy and moves with a springy hop characteristic of the group. It is a regional endemic, which inhabits the Cordillera Central and Cordillera de Talamanca above c.2000m.

WHITE-LORED GNATCATCHER *Polioptila albiloris* 11cm (4.25in)

A small grey bird with white underparts and a relatively long tail conspicuously edged with white, which it wags continuously. Males have black caps whilst females have grey ones. The male is shown in his non-breeding plumage when there is a white stripe from the base of the bill to above the eye. They prefer areas of scrubland and forest edges where they busily glean small invertebrates, usually in pairs. Inhabits the northwestern lowlands up to c.750m. The Tropical Gnatcatcher *Polioptila plumbea* is similar but their ranges barely overlap.

LONG-BILLED GNATWREN *Ramphocaenus melanurus* 12cm (4.75in)

The long, slender bill with a small terminal hook is the most distinctive feature of this species. It also has a longish tail, the feathers of which are white tipped and which it wags as it forages. It has skulking, wren-like habits so can be difficult to see in the dense forest edges it inhabits but attracts attention by its song, which is a prolonged trill. It can be found throughout the country in lowlands up to c.1200m though is less numerous in drier parts.

LONG-TAILED SILKY-FLYCATCHER *Ptilogonys caudatus*
male 24cm (9.5in), female 21cm (8.25in)

This appealing grey-blue and yellow bird has a distinctive tall crest and a long, black tail. The female is duller with more olive colouring. They are mostly seen around the tops of trees, frequently on exposed perches. They fly out to catch insects often achieved after acrobatic chases, but also descend to lower levels for berries. Usually seen in loose groups. They are found in Cordillera Central and Cordillera de Talamanca from c.1800m to high elevations. A regional endemic.

BLACK-AND-YELLOW SILKY-FLYCATCHER *Phainoptila melanoxantha* 21cm (8.25in)

Male (above); female (right)

The male of this species is black with yellow rump, breast and flanks and a grey belly. The female is less distinctive with black confined to her cap. Her face is grey, back olive-green but grading to more yellow on the rump, and underside olive-green. Inhabits highland forests and clearer surrounding areas feeding mainly on berries but also insects, which they glean from foliage or catch in flight. They can be seen alone or in small loose groups throughout the country at elevations above c.1200m. A regional endemic.

RED-EYED VIREO *Vireo olivaceus* 14cm (5.5in)

This species is a migrant passing between North and South America so can be very common in the fall and spring. It is olive-green on its back and wings, pale below with a hint of yellow on the flanks. Has a substantial bill with a small hook on the tip, a grey cap edged with a black stripe, a white stripe above the eye and a dark stripe through it. The iris is red. Forages in loose groups feeding on fruit and insects, generally in the lowlands. The Yellow-green Vireo *Vireo flavoviridis* is very similar but has more yellow on its sides and lacks the black border to its cap.

BANANAQUIT *Coereba flaveola* 9cm (3.5in)

A small, active bird with a characteristically short, sharply-pointed, down-curved bill. Its plumage is mostly dark grey above, yellow below, with a conspicuous white stripe above the eye, and a grey throat. It feeds on nectar, often by piercing the base of large flowers, and also forages acrobatically among foliage searching for insects and juicy fruit. It is found in a wide range of wooded habitats and can often be seen in mixed species flocks of foraging birds, particularly on the Caribbean slope and the southern part of the Pacific slope.

TENNESSEE WARBLER *Vermivora peregrina* 11.5cm (4.5in)

An undistinguished warbler with olive-green plumage on its upperparts, and white to pale yellow underparts. It has a pale stripe above the eye and a dark one through it, and some have a pale wing-bar. The male has a grey head during the breeding season. They forage for insects and nectar in the forest canopy and edges of fairly open areas such as plantations and gardens. They are winter visitors and passage migrants so are most abundant in autumn and spring when they can be seen throughout the country though rarely at high altitudes. Wintering birds favour altitudes up to c.2000m on both slopes.

CHESTNUT-SIDED WARBLER *Dendroica pensylvanica*
11.5cm (4.5in)

Male, breeding (left); male, non-breeding (right)

This is a lively bird with a slender, pointed bill. The male breeding plumage is distinctive because of his yellow cap, black stripes on face and back and chestnut flanks. In winter plumage is similar to the female with olive-green back, greyish-white underparts, the chestnut restricted to bands on his side, and double yellow bars on the wing. They forage at all levels of trees and shrubs for insect prey and fruit in forested areas on both slopes except at the highest levels and in driest areas. Probably the commonest North American migrant warbler to winter in rain forest in the lowlands and mid-elevations. Moult into breeding plumage before migrating back north.

GREY-CROWNED YELLOWTHROAT *Geothlypis poliocephala*
13.5cm (5.25in)

The male's mask is much smaller than in other yellowthroats and the only black on the female's face is restricted to in front of the eye. The male has a grey cap and is olive-green above and yellow below. The female is generally browner except for her yellow throat. Forages for invertebrates in meadows, savannahs and other grassy areas and also takes some berries. Inhabits the lowlands of both slopes up to c.1500m. Range is increasing with deforestation.

WILSON'S WARBLER *Wilsonia pusilla* 11cm (4.25in)

The black cap on the male distinguishes him from other small, yellow warblers. The female is similar but lacks the black cap which leaves her difficult to differentiate from some other female warblers: particularly Hooded Warbler *Wilsonia citrina* (larger, white on outer tail), Yellow Warbler *Dendroica petechia* (lacks bright yellow forehead and face but has yellow edges on wings and tail). Wilson's Warbler is an active species flitting about the canopy, clearings and forest edges in search of small insects. Although seen in most areas when on migration, as a winter resident it is probably commonest in highlands.

SLATE-THROATED REDSTART *Myioborus miniatus* 12cm (4.75in)

This distinctive warbler has a rufous-red crown and outer tail feathers tipped with white and often displays them by fanning its tail. It flits actively about the middle levels of highland forests often behaving like a flycatcher with acrobatic aerial chases after flying insects. It also forages at edges and clearings of forests and surrounding areas. It is common in humid mid-elevations on both slopes.

COLLARED REDSTART *Myioborus torquatus* 12.5cm (5in)

Its bright yellow face and rufous crown make this a distinctive bird. Its back, wings and tail are grey to black and its belly is yellow with a dark grey breast band. The tail has white edges and it has the habit of displaying them by fanning its tail feathers. It favours cloud forest and adjacent areas including pastures and often forages with mixed species flocks in search of its insect prey. It is a common resident usually above 1600m, from the mountains of Cordillera de Tilarán south. An area endemic.

114

THREE-STRIPED WARBLER *Basileuterus tristriatus* 13cm (5in)

This warbler has an unusual pattern of stripes on its head, as shown in the photograph. Otherwise it lacks distinctive characters with olive upperparts and pale yellow underparts that are tinged with olive on the breast. It forages in small family groups which continuously call back and forth to each other or with mixed species flocks. It can be found in forest understorey, both primary and mature secondary growth, including at their edges. Favours mid-elevations, 1000–2200m, mainly on the Caribbean side.

BUFF-RUMPED WARBLER *Phaeothlypis fulvicauda* 13cm (5in)

The rump and much of the tail is pale buff made conspicuous by the contrast with the brown plumage of the back and the frequent fanning and wagging of the tail. Underparts are also pale buff and there is a pale stripe over the eye. Found in the shady vicinity of rivers and streams, where it feeds on small invertebrates, taken from the ground and occasionally in flight. Occurs in lowlands up to c.1000m of the Caribbean slope and the south Pacific slope.

MONTEZUMA OROPENDOLA *Psarocolius montezuma*
male 50cm (20in) female 38cm (15in)

This is the larger of the two Oropendolas that occur in Costa Rica and has a chestnut back and a dark head with a blue skin patch. Its bill is bicoloured, black at the base, orange at the tip and extends back to the forehead. The bill shape gives this group its characteristic outline. A social bird, vocal and conspicuous especially at breeding colonies where long pendulous nests hang in high trees, sometimes 50 or more together. It takes advantage of a wide range of food sources including small vertebrates, invertebrates, fruit, seeds and nectar. Most easily seen in the Caribbean lowlands.

SCARLET-RUMPED CACIQUE *Cacicus uropygialis*
male 23cm (9in) female 20cm (8in)

This is a gregarious bird that forages in small, noisy groups, including mixed species flocks, but nests alone. It has a heavy but sharply pointed pale bill and pale blue eyes. Its plumage is a uniform black with bright red rump which is not always easy to see and which can make it difficult to tell apart from the Yellow-billed Cacique *Amblycercus holosericeus*. This latter species has a yellow eye, a longer tail and prefers a dense understorey habitat. The Scarlet-rumped Cacique inhabits the lowlands of the Caribbean and south Pacific slopes.

MELODIOUS BLACKBIRD *Dives dives*
male 25.5cm (10in), female 23cm (9in)

This is the only Costa Rican blackbird that is entirely black with a dark eye (Bronzed Cowbird *Molothrus aeneus* has red eye, is smaller and has proportionately smaller bill and tail). The female is duller, less glossy and with a tinge of brown. This species prefers semi-open country and edges of forest, pasture and streams and is a generalist feeder. Usually seen in pairs frequently calling back and forth to each other. First arrived in Costa Rica in the 1980s and has been expanding its range southwards ever since. Now occurs south of Río Tarcoles but is still most easily seen in the northwest.

GREAT-TAILED GRACKLE *Quiscalus mexicanus*
male 43cm (17in), female 33cm (13in)

The male is a large, all-black bird with a clear yellow eye. The female is a brown version, paler below, with a pale stripe above the eye and a shorter tail. Both have slightly down-curved bills and large, graduated tails. This is a very social bird which forages mostly on the ground, is more or less omnivorous and often considered a pest. Nests and roosts in groups. Their range has been expanding and it is now found countrywide up to mid-elevations.

BLACK-COWLED ORIOLE *Icterus dominicensis* 19cm (7.5in)

As is common in the orioles this species is black and yellow with the yellow featuring on the shoulder, belly and from the rump up to the lower back. Immatures have the black restricted to a face mask and throat. It forages, gleaning and probing actively, among the foliage of forest borders, plantations, along streams and also more open habitats, taking insects, nectar and berries. Roosts in large groups in areas of tall grass. They can be found throughout the lowlands of the Caribbean slope.

SPOTTED-BREASTED ORIOLE *Icterus pectoralis* 21cm (8.25in)

A largely yellow oriole with black upper back, throat, tail and wings. Black spotting on the breast is diagnostic and there are conspicuous white wing patches. The spotting differentiates it from the rather similar Streaked-backed Oriole (see opposite). Inhabits open, dry woodland, including around habitation. Forages for insects and nectar. Often seen in small flocks outside the breeding season. Found in the lowlands and foothills of the north Pacific slope, particularly around Golfo de Nicoya.

NORTHERN (BALTIMORE) ORIOLE *Icterus g. galbula* 18cm (7in)

The male of this oriole is mostly a vivid orange to yellow-orange with a black head and upper back and wings. The wings have white barring. The female is less striking and has a paler orange on her underparts, with olive-brown upperparts speckled in black on her crown, throat and back. She has two white wing bars. They prefer semi-open habitats where they glean for fruits, invertebrates and nectar. They are passage migrants and winter visitors on both slopes up to c.1500m and occasionally higher. Northern Oriole is now split into 2–3 species of which this one is known as Baltimore Oriole.

STREAKED-BACKED ORIOLE *Icterus pustulatus* 19cm (7.5in)

The diagnostic feature for this oriole is the black streaking on its orange-yellow back where most others species have solid black. Similar to Spotted-breasted Oriole (see opposite) but lacking spots on the breast. Confined to dry woodland, scrub and savannah where it feeds on insects gleaned from foliage plus fruit and nectar. Seen in family groups after nesting and can be found in the dry northwest of the Pacific slope.

RED-WINGED BLACKBIRD *Agelaius phoeniceus*
male 22cm (8.75in), female 18cm (7in)

The male is black with bright red epaulettes that have their lower edge fringed with buffy yellow. The female is smaller, brown, heavily streaked above and below with paler underparts. Favours marshes and waterside habitats where it forages for invertebrates. Also feeds on seeds, particularly on agricultural land where they can be a pest. Gregarious, particularly outside the breeding season when they form large flocks and roost communally. A common resident in the Pacific north west and northern Caribbean slope. Its range is extending.

RED-BREASTED BLACKBIRD *Sturnella militaris* 16.5cm (6.5in)

The male fits his name as he is a black bird with a red breast and throat. The female is largely brown with dark streaks and with pink on the breast. This species forages in open, wet areas for invertebrates, seeds and occasionally fruit. Gregarious, particularly in the non-breeding season. Breed in lowlands of the southern Pacific slope but range further north at other times. First arrived in Costa Rica from the south in 1974 but now occur as far north as the Sarapiquí lowlands on the Caribbean slope. Their range continues to expand.

GOLDEN-BROWED CHLOROPHONIA *Chlorophonia callophrys*
13cm (5in)

Female (above); male (right)

This species is a brilliant green and yellow and has a characteristic stubby bill. The female has similar colouring but is not quite as bright with less yellow and blue on the head and lacking the black breast stripe. Forages in small flocks except during the breeding season and feeds mostly on fruit (chiefly mistletoe) and also some insects. Most often seen in the tops of trees in cloud forest and bordering areas. Inhabits the highlands of both slopes, descending to lower altitudes only when fruit are scarce. A regional endemic.

BLUE-HOODED EUPHONIA *Euphonia elegantissima*
11cm (4.25in)

Male (above); female (right)

These are exquisite little birds with stubby bills. Both the male and female have the characteristic pale blue crown and nape and rufous forehead but otherwise differ. The male's back is blue-black while the female's is olive-green. Feeds mainly on fruit including so many mistletoe berries they are important dispersers of the seeds. They favour the canopy of trees in highland forests but also forage at lower levels at edges and semi-open habitats. Found in the highlands on the Pacific slope during the breeding season but range to the Caribbean side at other times. Persecuted for the caged-bird trade.

YELLOW-THROATED EUPHONIA *Euphonia hirundinacea*
11cm (4.25in)

Male (above); female (right)

This is one of several blue and yellow euphonias of Costa Rica. The male is distinguished from most others by its yellow throat and from Thick-billed Euphonia *E. laniirostris* by having less yellow on the forehead. The female is olive-green above and yellow below, fading to white on the belly. Darker above and has a thicker bill than female White-vented *E. minuta*, while the female Thick-billed has no white on the belly. Eats mostly berries, especially mistletoe, and some insects. Favours the edges of woodland, plantations and semi-open areas from lowlands to c.1400m on both slopes, chiefly in the north.

OLIVE-BACKED EUPHONIA *Euphonia gouldi* 9.5cm (3.75in)

Male (above); female (right)

The male of this euphonia is glossy green above tinged with steely green-blue and with a conspicuous yellow forehead. The rufous belly of the male is flanked by olive-green sides. The female is olive-green above with a rufous forehead, more yellow below with rufous only on her undertail coverts. Often seen in pairs or small groups and associates with mixed flocks in search of small fruits and berries. Frequents the higher levels of forest trees coming lower at edges and in open areas. Found throughout the lowlands on the Caribbean slope.

SILVER-THROATED TANAGER *Tangara icterocephala* 13cm (5in)

This tanager is bright yellow below with black wings and tail, black stripes on the back, a glossy white throat and a black stripe down the side of the face. Both the wings and tail are edged with green-yellow. The female is similar but duller. Forages through the mid to high levels of trees in wet forests in search of fruit and insects, usually in small groups and often in mixed flocks. They can be found in humid forests on both slopes at elevations above c.600m but mostly on the Caribbean side.

GOLDEN-HOODED TANAGER *Tangara larvata* 13cm (5in)

This strikingly-coloured tanager has a yellow-buff head and a black mask edged with blue. Blue also appears on the sides and wings and the belly is white. It is a bird of the canopy in forests and more open wooded areas including secondary growth and gardens. Their predominant food is fruit and berries but they also glean for insects and occasionally catch them in flight. Found in the rain forests from lowlands up to c.1500m along the length of the Caribbean slope and in the south on the Pacific side. Also known as Golden-masked Tanager.

SPANGLED-CHEEKED TANAGER *Tangara dowii* 13cm (5in)

A dark bird with black head and back and diagnostic pale blue-green spotting round the sides of the head, which becomes more defined on the breast. It has a cinnamon belly, pale green rump and a small cinnamon patch on the crown. Feeds on fruits and small invertebrates from high levels of trees in wet mountain forests. Usually forages in pairs or small groups and often associates with mixed flocks. Inhabits altitudes between c.1000m–2750m throughout the highlands south to Panama, being absent from only the area north of Cordillera de Tilarán. This species is a regional endemic.

GREEN HONEYCREEPER *Chlorophanes spiza* 13cm (5in)

Male (above); female (right)

The predominant colour of the male is bright, glossy blue-green, darker on the wings and tail, with a black cap and face and a red iris. The bill has a dark upper mandible and yellow lower one and is slightly down-curved. The female is a much duller green, darker above and pale below. Inhabits tree tops and forest edges usually in pairs and often joins mixed flocks. Feeds on nectar, fruit and small insects. Common in the forests on the Caribbean and south Pacific slopes up to c.1000m.

SHINING HONEYCREEPER *Cyanerpes lucidus* 10cm (4in)

The male has rich blue and black colouring with a short tail and bright yellow legs. The female is largely green with blue restricted to a moustachial stripe and streaking on the breast. Seen in pairs and family groups and forages in mixed species flocks in the canopy and lower at forest borders. Feeds on nectar, fruit and insects often gleaned in acrobatic positions. Occurs in the lowlands and foothills the length of the Caribbean side and on the south Pacific slope.

BLUE DACNIS *Dacnis cayana* 11.5cm (4.5in)

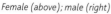

Female (above); male (right)

The male is a bright blue with black patches on the face, back, wings and tail. The female is largely green with blue restricted to her head. Usually forages in pairs or small groups, often with mixed flocks, and feeds on fruit, nectar and invertebrates. Forages at most levels including the canopy and lower at forest edges and clearings. Fairly common in lowlands and up to c.1200m on both slopes.

SCARLET-THIGHED DACNIS *Dacnis venusta* 12cm (4.75in)

The male is blue above, black below, and has red thighs. The female is blue-green above, buff below and has cinnamon thighs. This species usually forages as pairs or in family groups, often in mixed flocks. It favours rain forest canopy and edges and also more open areas if fruit is available. Inhabits foothills and up to c.1500m on the Caribbean and south Pacific slopes but ranges into lowlands after breeding if the fruit supply dictates it.

BLUE-GREY TANAGER *Thraupis episcopus* 15cm (6in)

This species is blue-grey all over but most brightly coloured on the wings and tail. The male is shown above; the female is essentially similar but rather greyer. Usually seen in pairs. This is a familiar and easily identified species that is generally seen in open areas, including towns and their suburbs, but also at forest edges. It is chiefly a fruit-eater but also takes nectar and insects. Found throughout the country at altitudes up to c.2300m but is least numerous in the dry northwest.

PALM TANAGER *Thraupis palmarum* 16cm (6.25in)

The greyish olive-green of this species can have a glossy grey sheen in some lights, as shown, but the black flight feathers are diagnostic of this tanager. Usually seen in pairs which occur in fairly open habitats with scattered trees such as parks, gardens and plantations. As their name suggests, they favour palms. They feed on fruits and also small invertebrates, which they glean from foliage or occasionally catch in flight. They can be found throughout the country up to elevations of c.1500m but are rare in the northwest.

SCARLET-RUMPED TANAGER *Ramphocelus passerinii* 16cm (6.25in)

The male is unmistakable with his brilliant red lower back and rump contrasting with the velvet black of the rest of his plumage. This species has now been split into two and the main differences are evident in the females. The female of Cherrie's Tanager *R. costaricensis* having brighter orange on the breast and rump. The Cherrie's male has a more orangey red on his back and rump. They frequent semi-open areas including gardens, often in mixed flocks, and feed on fruit and insects. Both inhabit lowlands to mid-elevations, Scarlet-rumped on the Caribbean slope, Cherrie's on the south Pacific slope.

Female (above); male (right)

SUMMER TANAGER *Piranga rubra* 16.5cm (6.5in)

Male (above); female (right)

The male is entirely red, darker on the wings with a prominent, thick, pale bill. The female is olive-brown above and yellow-olive below with a hint of ochre, brightest at the under tail coverts. Also has a thick, pale bill but the upper mandible is darker than the male's. A migrant and winter visitor that ranges through a variety of habitats from the canopy of forests, to second growth, fields and gardens, feeding on fruit and invertebrates. A resident countrywide between September and April from lowlands to c.2500m on both slopes.

BLACK-CHEEKED ANT-TANAGER *Habia atrimaxillaris* 18cm (7in)

This is a generally dark grey bird with a darker face, a partly concealed salmon-pink crown-patch and a wash of salmon on the underparts, particularly the throat. The female is similar but duller, with a smaller crown-patch. Frequents the understorey of lowland forest and feeds on insects and fruit. Forages in pairs and small groups, joins mixed flocks and occasionally follows ant swarms. This is a Costa Rican endemic with a range restricted to the dense forests of the Osa Peninsula and Golfo Dulce. It is increasingly threatened by the disappearance of its favoured habitat.

COMMON BUSH-TANAGER *Chlorospingus ophthalmicus*
13.5cm (5.25in)

This is a largely olive-green bird with a grey-brown head and white in the centre of the belly. The conspicuous white patch behind the eye is diagnostic and distinguishes it from the similar Ashy-throated Bush-Tanager *C. canigularis*. It is a noisy, active bird that forages at many levels, but chiefly low, in wet, highland forests. It joins mixed flocks foraging for fruit and insects. Very common and found in forested areas above 400m on the Caribbean slope and above 1100m on the Pacific slope but rare above 2300m.

SOOTY-CAPPED BUSH-TANAGER *Chlorospingus pileatus*
13.5cm (5.25in)

This bird's distinctive head pattern differentiates it from the Common Bush-Tanager (see above). The head is black with a broad white stripe above the eye, which is broken or appears kinked, and a white chin and throat sparsely flecked with black. It forages busily among the epiphytes and foliage of highland forests in small scattered flocks. It feeds on small fruits, berries, insects and spiders and inhabits the highlands of Cordilleras de Tilarán, Central and Talamanca. A regional endemic.

BUFF-THROATED SALTATOR *Saltator maximus* 20cm (8in)

The buff on the throat is bordered in black, and the white stripe over the eye is conspicuous. The back and tail are olive-green. It feeds on invertebrates, fruit and nectar found in plantations, residential areas, meadows and forest edges. Usually seen in pairs which have a melodious contact call. Often joins mixed flocks and is found throughout the country up to altitudes of c.1500m but is rare in dry regions.

BLACK-FACED GROSBEAK *Caryothraustes poliogaster* 16.5cm (6.5in)

This stocky bird is olive-green on its back and wings with yellow head and breast and black face. The bill has a small hook at the tip and is paler at the base. The underparts and rump are grey. It is a bird that favours the tops of trees in wet forests and bordering areas and travels in loose noisy groups which attract attention with metallic calls. It feeds on fruit, nectar and insects. Inhabits lowland humid forests on the Caribbean slope up to an elevation of c.900m.

BLACK-THIGHED GROSBEAK *Pheucticus tibialis* 20cm (8in)

This is a largely yellow bird with black wings, back, thighs and tail and a small but conspicuous white wing patch. The black thighs are not always conspicuous in the field. A male is shown; females are similar but duller. Feeds on fruit, seeds and insects, which are gleaned from foliage or caught in flight. Occurs mainly above 1000m but some descend to lower elevations outside the breeding season. An area endemic.

BLUE-BLACK GROSBEAK *Cyanocompsa cyanoides* 16.5cm (6.5in)

This species has a massive, dark, conical bill. The male is glossy blue-black, the female is dark brown, slightly paler below. This species favours wet forest undergrowth, both primary and secondary, and bordering areas. The main diet is seeds and fruit but also gleans for insects. Usually seen in pairs and occasionally in a mixed species flock. Inhabits the lowlands and foothills of the Caribbean and south Pacific slopes.

YELLOW-FACED GRASSQUIT *Tiaris olivacea* 10cm (4in)

The male is olive-green with distinctive yellow markings on the face and chin, bordered in black. The female is more uniformly olive-green but paler at the throat and on a stripe over the eye. Has a short, conically shaped bill suitable for eating seeds that form the bulk of its diet, but also gleans for insects. Common in open grassy areas such as fields and verges on the Caribbean and south Pacific slopes up to altitudes of c.2000m. Rare in the northwest.

VARIABLE SEEDEATER *Sporophila aurita* 10.5cm (4in)

L to R: Caribbean race male; Pacific race male; Pacific race female

There are two races of this species in Costa Rica. The Caribbean male is almost all black except for white wing linings and small white wing patches. The Pacific male has considerably more white on the underparts and rump and a white collar. Both females are olive-brown with white wing linings. The Pacific race is shown; the Caribbean is more uniform olive-brown below lacking the almost white belly. A bird of semi-open grasslands, gardens and forest edges feeding on seeds and berries plus some insects, often in mixed species flocks. Common throughout the lowlands and foothills of the Caribbean slope and southern Pacific slope.

BLUE-BLACK GRASSQUIT *Volatinia jacarina* 10cm (4in)

Female (above); male (right)

The male is blue-black all over. The female is largely brown, darker above, paler below but streaked. This species inhabits open, grassy areas where it tends to forage inconspicuously among the vegetation. The male makes himself more conspicuous in the breeding season when he displays, simultaneously singing and jumping from his perch. Feeds chiefly on seeds but also fruit and invertebrates. Found commonly throughout the country in lowlands and foothills.

PEG-BILLED FINCH *Acanthidops bairdii* 13.5cm (5.25in)

The male (shown) is entirely slate grey, paler on the underparts. The female is grey-brown, paler below and faintly streaked. Both sexes have the distinctive bill which is narrow, pointed and slightly tilted up. The upper mandible is black and the lower yellow (less bright on the female). This is a bird of the highlands which prefers forest edges and dense vegetation around more open habitats. It particularly favours bamboo thickets and feeds on nectar, small invertebrates, seeds and berries. It lives chiefly above c.2000m to the tree line, from Cordillera de Tilarán south to Panama, but descends to lower altitudes during the rainy season. A regional endemic.

SLATY FLOWERPIERCER *Diglossa plumbea* 10cm (4in)

Male (left); female (above)

The peculiar up tilted bill shape of this small bird gives it a distinctive outline. The hooked upper mandible is used to grip a flower while the sharp lower mandible pierces and opens it so the brush-tipped tongue can be inserted to steal nectar. The male is a fairly uniform grey while the female is brown, lightly streaked below. Forages actively, alone or in pairs, in shrubby forest edges and clearings and bordering areas including páramo. Feeds on insects as well as nectar and can be found commonly in highlands throughout the country. An area endemic.

LARGE-FOOTED FINCH *Pezopetes capitalis* 20cm (8in)

This is a large, dark finch, which is olive-green with a black head and slaty grey stripes on the crown. It is largely ground dwelling and really does have large feet though this is not always obvious in the field. When foraging this species scratches the ground vigorously, with both feet at once, in search of seeds and insects. Inhabits forest thickets and edges at altitudes above c.2000m the length of the country, including páramo. A regional endemic occurring in only Costa Rica and western Panama.

YELLOW-THIGHED FINCH *Pselliophorus tibialis* 18.5cm (7.25in)

The conspicuous puffy yellow feathers of its thighs make this finch distinctive. It is otherwise dark grey with a black head, wings and tail. It forages at any level of the highland wet forests it inhabits and feeds on invertebrates and berries. Mostly seen as pairs or in small, noisy family groups, which may also associate with mixed species flocks. It inhabits the highlands of Cordilleras de Tilarán, Central and Talamanca, generally above c.1500m up to the tree line. It is an area endemic, occurring in only Costa Rica and western Panama.

CHESTNUT-CAPPED BRUSH-FINCH *Atlapetes brunneinucha* 18.5cm (7.25in)

The head pattern of this species is distinctive with its chestnut cap, black face, white throat and three small white spots on the forehead. There is a black breast band above grey belly and the back is dark olive-green. It forages mostly on the ground in the undergrowth of wet forests where it flicks aside leaf litter in search of invertebrates but also forages for insects and berries from low foliage. It is common but inconspicuous in rain forests between c.1000–2500m on both slopes.

ORANGE-BILLED SPARROW *Arremon aurantiirostris* 15.5cm (6in)

The bold black and white pattern on the head and breast of this sparrow is made even more striking by the bright orange bill. The upperparts are a less distinctive olive-green with a small yellow patch on the shoulder; the belly is white with grey flanks. This species favours the ground and understorey of wet forests where it forages in pairs or family groups in search of the invertebrates and berries on which it feeds. It can be found in the lowlands and foothills of the entire Caribbean slope and the south of the Pacific slope.

BLACK-STRIPED SPARROW *Arremonops conirostris* 16.5cm (6.5in)

The black stripes of its name appear on the head of this species. Its back is olive-green with an inconspicuous yellow patch on the shoulder. The underparts are pale grey with a white throat. It forages on the ground and at low levels in shrubs in fields, gardens, and plantations in the humid lowlands of the Caribbean slope and the south Pacific slope. Similar to the smaller Olive Sparrow *Arremonops rufivirgatus* which occurs only in deciduous woodlands of the north Pacific slope. There is no overlap in the ranges of the two species.

STRIPED-HEADED SPARROW *Aimophila ruficauda* 18cm (7in)

This is one of the larger sparrows and it has black and white stripes on its head. The upperparts are buff with the back and wings streaked with black, while the underparts are white to pale grey. It inhabits relatively open, scrubby areas and the edges of woodland where it forages on the ground for seeds, supplemented with small invertebrates. Mostly seen in small flocks and found only in the lowlands and foothills of the dry north Pacific slope.

RUFOUS-COLLARED SPARROW *Zonotrichia capensis* 13.5cm (5.25in)

The striped head, small crest, white throat and rufous collar give this sparrow a distinctive air. It is found commonly in areas of habitation such as gardens and parks and also in fields and secondary growth. It forages mainly on the ground in search of seeds and occasional insects and is often seen in pairs or small flocks. It is abundant throughout the country, including the centre of San José, above 600m and can occasionally be seen at lower levels.

GLOSSARY

c. Abbreviation of circa meaning 'approximately'.

Cere An area of skin surrounding the nostrils, at the base of the upper mandible of the beak.

Endemic An endemic is a species restricted to a defined area. Costa Rica has three species of birds that can definitely be found in Costa Rica alone. There are many more species that are restricted to the highlands that extend from Costa Rica to the Chiriqui Mountains of Panama. These species are referred to as **area or regional endemics**.

Epiphyte, epiphytic An epiphyte is a plant that grows on another plant, such as a tree, but does not receive any nourishment from it. They are a common feature of rain forests and include plants such as mosses, orchids and bromeliads.

Eye-ring Area immediately surrounding the eye.

Eyeshine Some nocturnal animals have a tapetum, a reflective layer in the eye, which enhances night vision. Light reflected from the back of an eye at night, e.g. in the light of a torch, can give a brilliant shine. The colour of the shine can assist identification as with Pauraque (ruby-red) or the Common Potoo (orange).

Eye-stripe A stripe of a particular colour that runs over/through the eye rather than above or below it.

Gleans/Gleaning Used by birdwatchers to refer to the systematic searching for and collecting of food items from among vegetation.

Invertebrates Animals without backbones including insects, molluscs (e.g. snails) and spiders. Marine invertebrates include such things as crabs, shrimps and shellfish.

Mandible The upper and lower mandibles comprise the bill or beak.

Mollusc A soft bodied invertebrate which usually has a hard, protective shell e.g. snail, limpet, or mussel.

Moult The shedding of old feathers and growth of new ones.

Moustachial Stripe Stripe of a particular colour running from the base of the bill down the side of the throat.

Páramo This is a habitat that occurs above the tree line and below the snow line resulting in a treeless area of low growth.

Primaries Flight feathers of the outer wing joint, see diagram on page 4.

Rain forest An area of forest, which receives high levels of rainfall. Although there may be seasonal variations in the amount of rain, the area does not dry out at any time of the year.

Sally/Sallies/Sallying Used here for when a bird suddenly flies out after prey and for fruit from a perched position.

Savannah Grasslands with scattered trees.

Secondaries Flight feathers of the inner portion of the wing. See diagram on page 4.

Species A species is a group of individuals with the same characteristics, which reproduce with each other.

Territorial Defends a particular area in order to protect a resource, such as food, nest or display area.

Trapliner Used to describe a feeding strategy utilized by some hummingbirds, where they exploit widely dispersed, nectar-rich flowers, visiting them on a regular circuit. By the time a flower is visited on a subsequent round it has replenished its nectar supply.

Undertail Coverts Small feathers which cover the bases of the tail feathers beneath the tail. See diagram on page 4.

Uppertail Coverts Small feathers which cover the bases of the tail feathers above the tail. See diagram on page 4.

Wing Coverts Small feathers which cover the bases of the primaries and secondaries. See diagram on page 4.

FURTHER READING

Burton, Robert, *The World of Hummingbirds*, Firefly Books, 2001

Fogden, Michael & Patricia, *Wildlife of the National Parks and Reserves of Costa Rica*, Fundacion Neotropica, 1997

Fogden, Michael & Patricia, *Hummingbirds of Costa Rica*, Fundacion Neotropica, 2005

Janzen, Daniel, Ed., Costa Rican Natural History, University of Chicago Press, 1983

Stiles, F. Gary & Skutch, Alexander F., *A Guide to the Birds of Costa Rica*, Christopher Helm, 1989

Exploring Costa Rica, The Tico Times, produced annually

USEFUL ADDRESSES

Costa Rica Tourism Institute (ICT)
Plaza del Cultura
San José
www.tourism-costarica.com

INDEX